INSIGHT POCKET GUIDES

Tenerife

GW00722670

APA PUBLICATIONS

Part of the Langenscheidt Publishing Group

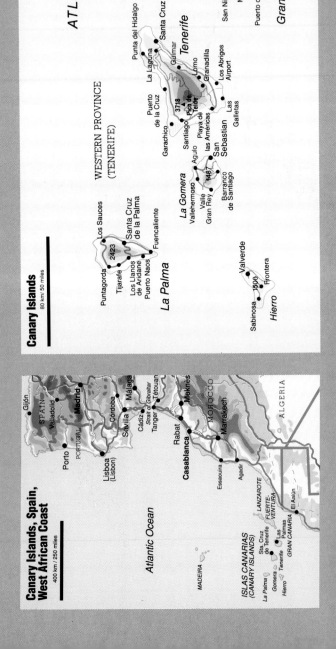

Canary Islands, Spain, West African Coast

400 km / 250 miles

Atlantic Ocean

MADEIRA

ISLAS CANARIAS (CANARY ISLANDS)

La Palma
Gomera ⌇ Tenerife
Hierro ⌇ Tenerife

LANZAROTE
FUERTE-VENTURA
Las Palmas
GRAN CANARIA

SPAIN

Gijón
Valladolid
Madrid

PORTUGAL
Porto
Córdoba
Sevilla
Málaga
Lisboa (Lisbon)
Cádiz
Strait of Gibraltar
Tanger
Tétouan
Rabat
Meknès
Casablanca
MOROCCO
Marrakech
Essaouira
Agadir
El Aaiun
ALGERIA

Canary Islands

80 km / 50 miles

ATLANTIC OCEAN

WESTERN PROVINCE (TENERIFE)

La Palma

Puntagorda
Los Sauces
Tijarafe
2423
Santa Cruz de la Palma
Los Llanos de Aridane
Puerto Naos
Fuencaliente

La Gomera

Vallehermoso
Agulo
1487
Valle Gran Rey
Barranco de Santiago
San Sebastian

Tenerife

Punta del Hidalgo
La Laguna
Santa Cruz de Tenerife
Güimar
Garachico
Puerto de la Cruz
3718 ▲ Pico de Teide
Santiago
Lomo
Granadilla
Los Abrigos
Airport
Playa de las Américas
Las Galletas

Hierro

Valverde
1500
Sabinosa
Frontera

Gran Canaria

Gáldar
Arucas
Las Palmas de G.C.
Teide
San Bartolome
Arinaga
San Agustin
San Nicolas
Mogán
Puerto de Mogán
Maspalomas

Welcome!

Tenerife is justly popular as a sunshine holiday destination, but few visitors realise that beyond the big hotels of its resorts lies a wild and beautiful island. Dominated by the peak of El Teide, it soars from sea to snow in a wild mix of rocky desert, lush valleys, fragrant forests and volcanic mountains. With its distinctly different north and south coasts, Tenerife offers great rewards for travellers who like to explore.

Whether you intend to hire a car, join excursions or just lie on the beach, the following pages written by Insight Guides' expert on Tenerife will meet your needs. As well as offering a series of mapped itineraries taking you to the remote corners of the island, this book guides you through the cities and resorts, pointing out their historic sights and recommending the best places for dining, shopping and entertainment.

Nigel Tisdall, a freelance writer based in Britain, has been visiting Tenerife for many years. For him the appeal of the island is much as it was in the days of the Romans, who knew the seven Canary Islands as the 'Isles of the Blessed'. In their eyes the archipelago was a fabled paradise graced by a benign climate, rich soil and wild fruit in such abundance that it could 'nourish an idle people without work or effort'. Looking at the crowds of sunbathers lying on the beaches of Tenerife today, it seems that nothing much has changed in 2,000 years.

C O N T E N T S

Dining, Shopping & Entertainment

Calendar of Events

Practical Information

All the essential background information you are likely to need, from taxis to tipping, climate to consulates.

Maps

Pages 8/9:
Tinerfeño dancers

HISTORY

Twenty million years ago, as the great plates of rock that form the Earth's crust drifted apart, the first Canary Islands were born, nosing out of the Atlantic as magma burst to the surface in a roar of volcanoes. Lanzarote and Fuerteventura led the way with the younger islands following westward – Tenerife was formed around ten million years ago while La Palma and El Hierro erupted some eight million years later.

A rough triangle covering almost 800 square miles (2,072 square kilometres), Tenerife's spectacular jumble of landscapes result from a succession of violent eruptions that have dramatically remodelled the island. Its two northern corners, the western Macizo de Teno and

the eastern Anaga peninsula represent its oldest parts – ancient basaltic lavas now sliced deep by erosion to form jagged ridges and valleys. Between them rises Spain's highest mountain, El Teide (12,195ft, 3,718m), a young strato-volcano that has added its own stony gore to these earlier lavascapes. Today its steep northern flanks, long watered by trade winds from the north-east, are lush and fertile while its southern foothills, now furrowed with *barrancos* (ravines), slope down to a dry, desert-like coastline.

The island's first inhabitants, the Guanches, found natural homes in the caves created by the lava-flows' contortions. Their arrival on the islands is a mystery, particularly as they appear to have had no knowledge of boat-building or even been able to swim. If they had a written language only

a few tantalising clues to it survive, enigmatic doodles scratched in the darkness of a cave wall or etched on the slate-smooth grey of a lava stream.

Despite their isolation the Guanches had a relatively advanced culture, fashioning tools and weapons from bone and wood and making *tabonas* (cutting-stones) from the sharp obsidian found beside Teide. In the summer they grazed pigs and goats in the vast crater (Las Cañadas) surrounding the volcano, later descending to the coastal valleys to harvest grain. According to the reports of the slave-traders and *conquistadores* who all but exterminated them, they were a noble and athletic people with 'strange idolatrous fancies'. The Guanches believed that an omnipotent god lived on Teide's summit and an evil one dwelt in its subterranean fires. They made primitive pottery and had sophisticated burial rites, elaborately mummifying their dead. The leather-wrapped skeletons of Guanches are still being found in caves on Tenerife and the Museo Arqueológico in Santa Cruz has some chilling examples.

Visitors to Tenerife often remark on the 'Guanche' features of a bus driver or pool attendant (a wide forehead and stocky build for example), but it's clear that by the start of the 16th century barely a thousand Guanches had survived the Spanish Conquest. If they did not die fighting the Spanish they were either abducted to the mainland or fell victim to newly-imported diseases.

The remainder were absorbed by the pioneer society that emerged as the

Left: El Teide volcano; Guanche rock art. Right: Guanche mummy

Spanish colonists settled, bringing Portuguese labour to work their new sugar plantations (see panel below).

In many ways the colonisation of the Canaries was a trial run for the *conquistadores'* greater exploits in the New World. Sugar production was soon established in those virgin lands, inevitably undercutting the Canarios' profitable trade with Europe. By then Tenerife's continued prosperity was assured, guaranteed by a strategic location on the busy sea-routes to America. The island became a smuggler's haven and in spite of a Spanish ban on slavery was used to corral African slaves prior to their long voyage across the Atlantic.

Tenerife's position also left it vulnerable to attack from pirates, attracted by the bullion ships that regularly called at Santa Cruz *en route* from Cuba or the Philippines. Over the years the port has proved a popular call for belligerent English fleets and ambitious naval commanders from Drake to Nelson have wreaked havoc in its harbour (see panel above). Most of the island's early fortifications were constructed in this lawless period – those still standing in-

---

Spain's Conquest of the Canary Islands

An ambitious Andalusian with a reputation for ruthlessness, Alonso Fernández de Lugo (1456–1525) completed the long conquest of the Canary Islands begun in 1402 by Jean de Béthencourt. After fighting in the six-year campaign to occupy Gran Canaria he found the Spanish Crown lacked the necessary resources to tackle La Palma and Tenerife and so turned to Genoese entrepreneurs for investment. He consequently seized La Palma with ease in 1492.

Two years later he landed on Tenerife with 1,000 men, marching straight into a trap set by the Guanches at the Barranco de Acentejo – now known as La Matanza (the massacre), 10 miles (16km) east of Puerto de la Cruz. Fortu-

nate to escape, De Lugo returned in 1495 with larger forces and was able to conquer the island mainly because of feuding between the native tribes. His victory took place at what is now La Victoria de Acentejo, open land where over 2,000 Guanches are said to have been massacred by the Spanish crossbows.

Rewarding his investors with land, De Lugo established lucrative sugar plantations in the north of Tenerife. In 1498 he married Beatriz de Bobadilla, reputedly the lover of Columbus but more usefully Countess of Gomera. When he died at the age of 69 De Lugo had amassed a considerable fortune, and changed 'The Fortunate Isles' forever.

Nelson's Attack on Santa Cruz

On 15 July 1797 Rear-Admiral Horatio Nelson (1758–1805) set sail from Cadiz with orders to seize 'the Town of Santa Cruz by sudden and vigorous assault'. His ostensible target was *El Principe d'Asturias*, a Spanish treasure-ship carrying bullion home from Manila, but the expedition was also motivated by Nelson's own quest for glory and the British desire for naval supremacy during the French Revolutionary Wars.

At midnight on 24 July Nelson launched his attack, leading 1,000 men ashore in a flotilla of small boats. In the heavy seas many missed their landing point and were dashed against the rocks, while others fell victim to fierce fire from the Castillo de San Cristóbal. Nelson was wounded in the right elbow by a cannon ball and forced to retreat. A small force did get ashore that night, capturing the Dominican convent close to the Iglesia de Nuestra Señora.

As dawn broke this party awoke to find themselves confronted by 8,000 Spanish troops. Their commanding officer promptly demanded an honourable retreat and in due course the local Comandante-General obliged, marching the British invaders back to their boats with bands playing. Gifts of wine and bread were sent with them, and Nelson returned the cordiality with English ale and cheese. Later the officers from both sides dined together and 25 British wounded were treated in the town hospital.

Altogether some 250 men were either drowned, killed or wounded and Nelson, who had already lost his right eye at Calvi, had his arm amputated. It was his only failure, and the captured ensigns hanging in the Museo Militar in Santa Cruz prove it.

clude the Castillo de San Felipe in Puerto de la Cruz and the Castillo de San Miguel in Garachico. In the old centre of La Laguna, the island's original capital, you can still walk the Renaissance grid of streets laid down by De Lugo. Many of Tenerife's first churches date from this time too, such as La Laguna's Cathedral (founded in 1515) and the Iglesia de Nuestra Señora de la Concepción (1502) – the latter still has a font once used by the Dominican monks to baptise the Guanches.

Discounting slaves, sugar marked the first in a succession of monocultures that have ruled Tenerife. Wine followed, the famous Malvasia beloved by the Elizabethan and Jacobean courts. 'But that,' the playwright Ben Jonson admitted, 'which most doth take my Muse, and me, is a pure cup of Canary wine.' By the end of the 17th century some 10,000 pipes of this sherry-like Sack were arriving in London annually, tasting something like today's fortified wines, Malmsey and Madeira.

Wine remained Tenerife's principal export well into the 18th century, stimulating the development of a cosmopolitan society on the island as European merchants settled in the Orotava valley. By then a *nouveau* aristocracy of Marquises and Counts led island life, residing in elegant palaces and Canary mansions that remain the most attractive architecture on Tenerife. Step into the cool interior courtyards of 17th-century mansions like the Casa de la Real Aduana in Puerto de la Cruz or the Casa de los Balcones in La Orotava, with their galleries of carved balconies overlooking plant-filled patios, and you are instantly back in these enlightened times. The Canary balcony, traditionally made from the native Canary pine, is the islands' best known decorative feature and still a common sight in many new houses. It reflects Tenerife's long history of fine wood-carving, exemplified by the magnificent 16th-century ceiling of La Laguna's Iglesia de Nuestra Señora de la Concepción. Weaving, needlework and pottery are other traditional island crafts – best seen at the Casa de Carta, an immaculately restored 18th-century country house that is now an outstanding ethnographical museum (on the Tacoronte-Valle Guerra road, open 10am–1pm, 4–7pm, winter 3–8pm, closed Fridays).

You may suspect that every church of significance on Tenerife is called 'Iglesia de Nuestra Señora de la Concepción' and you're not

Canary balcony

far wrong. Fortunately the Baroque version in La Orotava (1768) is unmistakeable, graced by a high dome and twin towers that proclaim the confidence and prosperity enjoyed by the island's ruling classes in the latter half of the 18th century. Its learned members went on to create the Jardín de Aclimatación de la Orotava in 1788, an experiment initiated by King Charles III with a view to accustomizing tropical plants to the climate of Spain.

Throughout the 19th century scholars, scientists and travellers took an increasing interest in Tenerife. The German naturalist Baron Alexander von Humboldt surveyed the Orotava Valley from what is now a famous *mirador* (viewpoint), exalting in its lush vegetation and later writing of the island's ability 'to banish melancholy and restore peace to a troubled spirit.' Botanists, natural historians and anthropologists re-discovered Tenerife and scientific explorers like Charles Piazzi Smyth – a future Royal Astronomer – scrambled up Teide to gaze at the stars.

Artists such as Elizabeth Murray and Marianne North visited, painting scenic panoramas that emphasised the Eden-like qualities of Tenerife's landscape and flora, and aroused considerable interest back home. Energetic adventurers toured the islands, like Olivia Stone, who claimed to be the first Englishwoman to visit El Hierro and wrote one of the Canary Islands' first travel guides, *Tenerife and its Six Satellites* (published in 1887).

Such enthusiasts paved the way for Tenerife's first tourists – by 1886 there were 500 a year – mostly gentlemen and lady travellers who climbed 'The Peak of Teneriffe' by mule, fortifying themselves with draughts of quinine and nonchalantly recording their exploits in journals.

By this time Santa Cruz had become the island's commercial and administrative centre, capital of an archipelago granted free trade status in 1822. The wine trade had finally collapsed, the casualty of wars in Europe and the Spanish American colonies and a series of diseases that ravaged the vineyards. Tenerife's farmers looked to cochineal as a replacement, introduced from Mexico in 1825. Prickly pears were planted to support the insect that produces this dye, but the development of synthetic dyes in the 1870s killed the infant trade.

Salvation eventually came in the shape of the small Canary banana, only introduced from China in 1855. Today its bright fronds still give a cheerful wave from many areas of Tenerife, a legacy of the 1880s when banana plantations were established on the island.

Banana workers, 1920

British companies like Fyffes and Yeowards dominated this huge trade, made possible by the advent of steamships and refrigerated shipping. Today the sweet Canary bananas are still exported to mainland Spain, though only with the help of government subsidies. Larger varieties from South America have commandeered the market and today the plantations are gradually being dug up and replaced with tourist complexes.

It was the regular services introduced by the banana and mail boats that brought the first 'package' tourists to Tenerife. Then, a 16-day round trip from Liverpool calling at Lisbon, Madeira, Las Palmas and Tenerife cost 10 guineas. In Puerto de la Cruz sumptuous hotels were built to accommodate the foreign visitors; European aristocracy regularly graced the croquet lawns and flower gardens of the biggest and best, the Grand Hotel Taoro (built in 1892), now a state-run casino.

These years also saw the establishment of the British community on the island (today it's officially 11,000 strong but certainly much

15

Historical Highlights

BC

3000 The island's first inhabitants, probably migrant tribes of Berber origin, pass through the Canary Islands leaving enigmatic rock inscriptions.

AD

1st century Pliny writes of an expedition sent by King Juba II of Mauritania to the islands. The explorers find many wild dogs there from which the Canaries may have got their name, *canis* being the Latin for dog.

2nd century By now the islands are settled by the Guanches, neolithic cave-dwellers thought to have arrived from North Africa.

1402 Jean de Béthencourt, a Norman lord backed by Henry III of Castile, launches a campaign to conquer the islands for the Spanish Crown.

1492 Columbus witnesses the eruption of Teide during his first voyage to the New World.

1496 De Lugo conquers Tenerife, the last Canary Island to fall to Spain.

16th–17th century Castilian and Portugese colonists mix with the surviving Guanches to create the ancestors of today's Tinerfeños. Wine becomes the principal export, the sweet Malvasia beloved of the Elizabethans.

1656 Admiral Blake wreaks havoc in Santa Cruz harbour, sinking 16 Spanish galleons carrying Mexican gold.

1706 An eruption of Teide destroys the port of Garachico, encouraging the development of what is now Puerto de la Cruz.

1723 Santa Cruz becomes the island capital. Attracted by the prosperous trade with the Americas, European merchants settle here and in the Orotava Valley, creating a thriving intellectual society.

1797 Nelson fails to take Santa Cruz during the French Revolutionary Wars.

1822 Santa Cruz is made the capital of the entire archipelago. As the wine trade declines, an attempt is made to replace it with cochineal production.

1852 The Canary Islands are declared a free trade zone. The advent of steamships and a growing trade with colonial Africa revives theeconomy.

1880 Banana plantations spread across the islands, controlled by fruit and shipping companies such as Fyffes and Yeowards. Steamships bring the first tourists to Puerto de la Cruz. Grand hotels are built to accommodate them.

1914 World War I destroys the banana boom. Many Canarios emigrate to South America.

1927 The Canary Islands are divided into two provinces administered from Santa Cruz (Tenerife, La Gomera, La Palma, El Hierro) and Las Palmas (Gran Canaria, Fuerteventura, Lanzarote).

1936 Francisco Franco, Comandante-General of the Canaries, flies from Tenerife to lead the military uprising that sparks off the Spanish Civil War (1936–9).

1959 Tourism offers an end to recession as direct flights to Tenerife commence; Puerto de la Cruz becomes an international resort.

1978 Reina Sofía airport opens on the Costa del Silencio, stimulating a second tourist boom centred on the resorts of Los Cristianos and Playa de las Américas.

1983 The Canary Islands are granted new powers of autonomy with their own constitution and elected representative bodies.

1986 Spain joins the EEC.

1995 Tenerife is now visited by over four million tourists a year.

larger) with its own Anglican Church, built in Puerto de la Cruz in 1890, soon followed by the British Games Club (1903).

World War I destroyed the banana trade at a stroke, forcing many Tinerfeños to seek better prospects in South America. Most emigrated to Cuba and Venezuela and

Franco in Tenerife, 1953

family ties with these countries remain strong, particularly on the smaller islands like La Gomera and El Hierro.

During the first half of the 20th century little was done to reverse the fortunes of the Canary Islands, a time of economic neglect punctuated by Franco's uprising in 1936 – launched from the islands – that led to the Spanish Civil War (see panel). Both the Germans and the Allies drew up plans to occupy the Canaries in the Second World War, but this was prevented by Franco's course of neutrality.

Franco's dictatorship continued until his death in 1975, a period of steady economic advance scarred by severe political and cultural repression. He visited Tenerife only once more, in 1953, but he helped develop the island through a programme of road building by the military. He also maintained the Canaries' free trade

Franco's Uprising

By March 1936 General Francisco Franco (1892–1975) had already been accused of involvement in several plots to establish a right-wing dictatorship in Spain. In an attempt to remove this threat the Republican government posted him to the Canary Islands. His term as Comandante-General there was to be short-lived, an uneasy prelude to the momentous civil war that would erupt four months later.

While on Tenerife, Franco survived three assassination attempts. He held clandestine meetings with fellow officers amid the cool pines of La Esperanza, and on 13 June the Tenerife garrison declared their allegiance at Las Raíces (The Roots). A stone obelisk now commemorates the site.

On 18 July Franco awoke to the news that the uprising had already begun in Spanish Morocco, a day earlier than planned. At 7am he broadcast his manifesto on Radio Tenerife, then flew to Tetuan, in northern Morocco, to take command of the rebel army.

By 20 July the Canaries were under his control: there was brief opposition in Tenerife and resistance on La Palma lasted a further eight days. Imprisonment and summary execution of Republicans ensued.

By the end of the year the Nationalists had taken over half of Spain, the start of a three-year Civil War that would claim up to a million lives. An imposing monument to its dead now dominates the Plaza de España in Santa Cruz.

status, enabling a diversification of agriculture that has now made Canary produce a familiar sight in European supermarkets. Today tomatoes, early potatoes, salad crops and flowers fly out of the island as the holidaymakers fly in.

Mass tourism began in the 1960s as direct flights to Los Rodeos airport enabled Europeans – principally British and German – to enjoy the guaranteed delights of Tenerife's winter sunshine. Despite the lack of good natural beaches and limited accommodation, resourceful schemes such as the Lago Martiánez complex enabled Puerto de la Cruz to develop as a major international resort. Within 10 years the number of beds available in the town rose dramatically from just 600 to a staggering 23,000.

A second wave of development followed the opening of a southern airport, Reina Sofía, in 1978. Hotels had already begun to appear around the fishing port of Los Cristianos and in the desert beside Playa de las Américas, but from then on the property market boomed.

Today the islanders are enjoying renewed prosperity, sharing the mainland's vitality as Spain throws away the dark memories of the Franco years. Granted new powers of regional autonomy, the Canarios are rediscovering their identity – the virulent graffiti you see on walls and roadsides by the radical separatist movement AWANAK is one expression of this. Some residents fear that the Canary Islands are losing their character and traditions, that islands like Tenerife will become an amorphous and predictable tourist ghetto. But long overdue improvements are also being made, particularly in the smaller western islands, inspired largely by the tourist industry and grants from the Spanish government and the EU. Unlike previous monocultures that simply exploited the islanders (in 1941 an unskilled agricultural labourer earned ten pesetas a day) the benefits of tourism are more widespread—for instance, on Tenerife the appetites of holidaymakers have kept the local fishing industry alive.

Now that the Canary Islands have successfully entered the modern world they are able to turn back to their traditions, albeit sometimes in a contrived fashion. Reawakened to the virtues of their 'Fortunate Island' many Tinerfeños are now making efforts, belatedly perhaps, to constrain the developers' free-for-all and dispel the lager lout image that has been the price of progress. Today the future is thought to lie up-market, in yacht marinas, golf courses and five-star hotels. Or it may not – the last major volcanic eruption in the Canary Islands was in 1971, on the neighbouring island of La Palma. Who's next?

Opposite: volcanic beach, El Médano

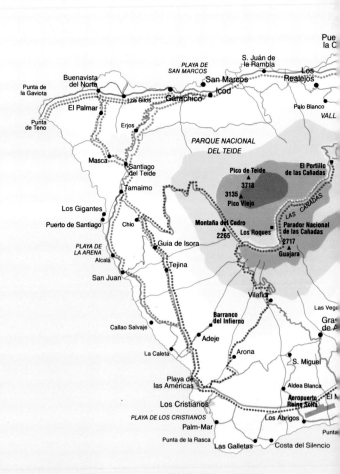

Tenerife

15 km

ATLANTIC OCEAN

Pue
la C

Punta de
la Gaviota

Buenavista
del Norte

PLAYA DE
SAN MARCOS

S. Juán de
la Rambla

Los
Realejos

San Marcos
Icod

Palo Blanco

VALL

Los Silos
Garachico

El Palmar

Erjos

PARQUE NACIONAL
DEL TEIDE

El Portillo
de las Cañadas

Masca

Pico de Teide
▲
3718

Santiago
del Teide

Tamaimo

3135 ▲
Pico Viejo

LAS CAÑADAS

Los Gigantes

Chio

Montaña del Cedro
▲
2265

Los Roques

Parador Nacional
de las Cañadas

Puerto de Santiago

LAS

PLAYA DE
LA ARENA

Alcalá

Guia de Isora

2717 ▲
Guajara

San Juan

Tejina

Vilaflor

Las Vega

Callao Salvaje

Barranco
del Infierno

Gra
de A

La Caleta

Adeje

Arona

S. Miguel

Playa de
las Américas

Aldea Blanca

Los Cristianos

Aeropuerto
Reina Sofía

El N

PLAYA DE LOS CRISTIANOS

Palm-Mar

Los Abrigos

Punta

Punta de la Rasca

Las Galletas

Costa del Silencio

Roque de Fuera

Roque de Dentro

PLAYA DEL ROQUE

Punta del Hidalgo

Bajamar   Punta del Hidalgo   Taganana

MONTE DE
LAS MERCEDES

Tejina

Tegueste

Mesa del Mar

Mirador Pico
del Inglés

Las Mercedes   Igueste

Guamasa

PLAYA DE
LAS TERESITAS

Tacoronte

Sauzal

La Laguna   S. Andrés

Aeropuerto
de los Rodeos

Matanza
Acentejo

Taco   Santa Cruz
de Tenerife

torla
ntejo

La Esperanza

Sobradillo

Mirador Pico
de las Flores

Santa Ursula

Las Raíces   S. Maria del Mar

ava

Mirador
de Oruño

Tabaiba

LAVA

amansa

Barranco
Hondo

Arafo

Las Arenitas

Candelaria

servatorio

Güimar

Puerto de Güimar

Mirador de
Don Martin

El Escobonal   Lomo de Mena

Zarza

PLAYA DE LA MARGALLERA

Fasnia   *PLAYA DE TOPUERQUE*

Icor

Arico El Nuevo

de   Poris de
Abona   Punta de Abona

ATLANTIC   OCEAN

del Camello

MEDANO

Guide to the Guide

Spend your first three days on Tenerife getting to know its spectacular volcanic scenery and remote mountain villages. The three itineraries here are each of a day's duration, and take you to dramatic peaks and superb coasts. In each case you can start you tour from either Playa de las Américas or Puerto de la Cruz.

Parque Nacional del Teide

El Teide is a relatively young, upstart volcano that arose one million years ago to become Tenerife's centrepiece and the highest mountain in Spain (12,195ft, 3,718m). Pushing imperiously through the clouds, it's also the high point of any trip to the island, a brutal, lava-streaked beauty that can still stir the imagination. Its peak soars above a vast crater known as the Circo de Las Cañadas, the collapsed shell of a much older and larger volcano, where a colossal rubble lies scattered as fresh as the day it was vomited. In this torched landscape of burnt rock and bright sunlight (a popular location for fash-

Above and left: views of El Teide

ion shoots and movies set in prehistoric times) Nature's power lies spectacularly petrified.

Despite its barren appearance, this No Man's Land is constantly changing. in winter Teide's slopes may glisten with snow and the rocks assume a life-denying pallor but come May the small sandy plateaux below the peak (Las Cañadas) spring to colour. Extremes of temperature and wind have produced a spectacular endemic flora that blooms briefly but brightly – suddenly the wilderness catches light as the Teide broom *retama del pico* bursts into pink and white flowers and the bright red, six-foot-tall (1.8m) *taginaste* (viper's bugloss) rises into the sky like a surreal scarlet umbrella.

Today the peak and its surrounding caldera are part of a conservation area, the **Parque Nacional del Teide**. The park covers 52.3 square miles (135.7 sq km) and, despite receiving over a million visitors every year you can find plenty of peaceful spots if you walk – take stout shoes, sunglasses, sun hat and something to drink. If you plan to climb to the summit you'll need to make an early start. Around El Portillo there are some *bar-restaurantes* but if you like to get away from the world take your own picnic.

To reach El Teide you have a choice of routes, depending on where you are based. Route 1 starts from Playa de las Américas; Route 2 from Puerto de la Cruz.

Take the main road east from **Playa de las Américas** to the Los Cristianos junction, where you turn north following signs for Arona (C882). Here you start the long climb towards Las Cañadas, turning left onto the TF511, by-passing Arona and up a serpentine series of bends that steadily rise through semi-cultivated terraces towards pine forest. On the way you'll notice the fields are covered in a light, volcanic gravel known as *picón*, used as a mulch to help retain moisture in the soil.

The road (TF5112) curls up to the lofty settlement of **Vilaflor,** where a sudden left turn takes you up to the **Mirador de San Roque** (by a small chapel) which gives wide views back over the fields to the coast. Just below the viewpoint is the **Restaurante El Mirador** which serves Canarian food and is a good place to return to on another occasion if you decide you want to enjoy a quiet meal away from the coastal resorts.

After taking in the view, return to the main road and turn left, skirting Vilaflor up to another viewpoint, the **Mirador de los Pinos**. Now you are in the heart of the pine forest where magnificent Canary pines tower above and the air is gloriously invigorating – if you cross the road here you will

Roadside shrine

find a signposted walk that will take you further into this aromatic Eden.

Further on up the road (C821) passes the source of Vilaflor mineral water, widely drunk throughout the Canary Islands. After this, a picnic site at **Las Lajas** is another inviting stop. At some point on your way up you will have to pass through the clouds, the mist and pine trees gradually thinning to reveal the rich colours of the mountain rocks and plants lit by bright sunshine.

The road twists and turns until suddenly you round a corner and confront **Teide** rising high in the sky. Cutting through the rough crater walls at **Boca de Tauce** you suddenly find yourself in the mysterious landscape of the Parque Nacional del Tiede (for the remainder of this itinerary, see *Exploring the Park, page 26*).

Teide finch

Make your way up to the *autopista* and then follow the signs to **La Orotava**. You want the the C821 (sometimes signposted to Las Cañadas) which will eventually lead you all the way to Teide. The road climbs through the historic town of La Orotava (*see Option 8, page 68*) and up into the famous **Orotava Valley**. Once a luscious sea of banana fronds and fruit trees, it's now liberally sprinkled with new houses, invariably unfinished.

Continue your ascent, carefully dodging the kamikaze children who sell eggs and fruit from the roadside. It's quite likely you will encounter a belt of thick mist – put your lights on and press ever onwards and upwards. In due course it will thin, revealing a glorious pine forest lit by bright sunshine. Banks of cloud may mask the valley below but up ahead it's heavenly.

Roques de García

Along the way there are several picnic sites and forest pull-ins. **Mirador de Margarita Piedra** is particularly interesting – across the road is a large volcanic bomb that has burst into the shape of a daisy *(margarita)*. Soon after here the road rises to confront the full majesty of Teide and the ancient pass of **El Portillo**. Continue straight ahead, into the spectacular wonderland of the **Parque Nacional del Teide**.

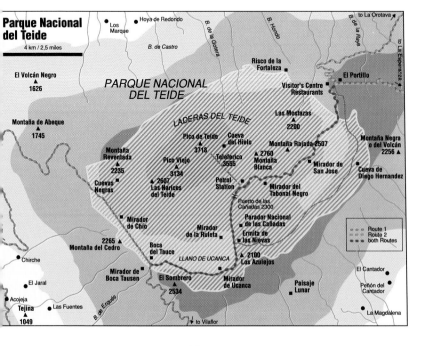

The Parque's most accessible areas lie to the south of Teide, united by a spectacular highway, the C821. This route through the Parque follows the C821 from Boca de Tauce in the west around to El Portillo in the east. If you have come from Puerto de la Cruz, you can either drive on to Boca de Tauce, where this itinerary starts (a distance of 12 miles/20km) or follow the itinerary in reverse.

At the **Mirador Boca de Tauce** there are clear views of Teide's dark side and of the older volcanic peak of **Pico Viejo** (10,286ft/ 3,135m) alongside the younger and higher **Pico de Teide.** Behind you rise the jagged crater walls known as the **Circo.** These mark the southern edge of the vast caldera which Teide now dominates.

Ten miles (16km) wide, this vast crater is thought to have been formed some three million years ago. One theory suggests a huge volcano covered the whole Parque, rising as high as 16,000ft (4,880m), which later collapsed to leave a giant crater of which only the southern walls remained visible after the eruption of Pico Viejo and El Teide two million years later. Another claims there were two craters, their dividing line now marked by the famous Roques de García further east.

The interior crater now comprises seven small, flat, gravel-like plains known as *cañadas*. On your way to these you pass the gloomy **Llano de Ucanca,** originally a lake, surrounded by dark lava. As you round the bend look for **Los Azulejos,** luminous rocks tinged a bright jade from copper oxide.

Shortly afterwards a small turn off to your left leads to the **Roques de García,** the most popular photo-opportunity in the Canaries. Every year hundreds of thousands of visitors come to see these rocks, sculpted into enigmatic shapes by erosion, where they take so many pictures you begin to wonder if they were secretly built by Kodak.

Opposite Las Roques is the **Parador Nacional de las Cañadas,** a state-owned hotel whose guests have the pleasure of seeing Teide after the tourist coaches have left. Most

Los Azulejos

people just pop in for a drink and to use the toilets but it's well worth staying overnight to sleep deep in the heart of a volcanic crater. At night the sky is peppered with stars and the dawn memorably unveils a new, pink Teide.

The Parador is a good place for a break and a useful base for a hike in Las Cañadas. To do this head back towards Los Azulejos, past the small *ermita* Nuestra Señora de las Nieves, and turn off down a path signposted **Camino de Chasna**. This was the old route linking Orotava and Vilaflor up which the Guanches would come in summer to graze their sheep and goats — you can still see their caves tucked in among the rocks and up in the crater walls. The walk actually continues right round to **El Portillo** (four hours) but don't do too much, as even here the air is thin and you quickly tire. Quite soon you'll lose the crowds and have only lizards, butterflies and silence for company. Here you can enjoy the colour and lunacy of this lava-strewn landscape and contemplate the might of that flamboyant monster, Teide.

From the Parador the road runs across the caldera to the foot of Teide, where a turn-off leads to the *Teleférico* (cable car); use

Climbing Teide

Every year some 300,000 people pant their way to Teide's summit. The prizes are great, the effort considerable. Those who conquer the volcano are rewarded with the stench of sulphur and dream-like views over Tenerife and other cloud-fringed islands: **Gran Canaria** to your east, **La Palma, La Gomera** and **El Hierro** to the west. On the way down you can fortify yourself with hot chocolate and brandy dispensed in the mountainside bar by **La Rambleta**.

A cable car covers most of the ascent — it only takes eight minutes but you'll have to queue in the sun for at least 1 1/2 hours before you get a ride. The earlier you can get there the better: up cars run daily 9am–4pm, last down 5pm, closed if windy. From here it's a breathtaking half-hour's walk/climb up another 560ft (170m) — literally, for here the air is rare and progress slow. Don't go if you are pregnant or suffer from heart or respiratory complaints. Strong shoes, a sun hat and sunglasses are essential, plus something warm — at that altitude it's still cold in spite of the sunshine.

Two short signposted walks also take you round Teide's flanks. One heads out for a view of **Pico Viejo's** crater and the other leads to the **Mirador La Fortaleza**—both allow close-up inspection of sulphurous fumaroles and fascinating lava formations.

More experienced climbers can take the steep three-hour ascent starting at **Montaña Blanca,** with the option of an overnight stay at **El Refugio de Altavista**. Do not set out without adequate preparation — for more details contact the Visitor's Centre.

the cable car if you intend to climb Tiede (see panel). The road then curls round three *montañas* with several pull-offs allowing you to stop and survey this almighty mess. **Mirador de Tabonal Negro** overlooks a choppy sea of liverish lava reminiscent of dog food. Some of these rocks are capped with the shiny black of obsidian, used by the Guanches to make *tabonas* or cutting-stones.

Next you will pass **Montaña Blanca**, the starting point for the longer walk to the summit – a short scramble up its pumice slopes is generally enough for most people. **Mirador de San José** follows, close to some pumice dunes known as **Arenas Blancas**. Montaña Rajada lies behind you while further on are the mustard slopes of Las Mostazas.

To get the best of the Parque pay a visit to the **Centro de Visitantes** near **El Portillo** (open daily 9am–4pm). This has visual displays and videos explaining the geology and volcanic history of Tenerife and the other Canary Islands, with a bookstall and information on Teide and its unique flora and fauna. The Centre has useful leaflets detailing the signposted trails you can follow and also runs free guided walks led by an English-speaking ranger. For further information, telephone 29 01 29.

For the return journey to the coast, you again have a choice of routes, given below.

1. From Teide down to Playa de las Américas via Chio

Returning to **Boca de Tauce** turn right onto the C823 towards **Chio**. This straight road runs along Teide's most melancholic side, a darkness of inhospitable lava-dribble that still shuns the advances of Tenerife's tenacious plantlife. At the **Mirador de Chio** you can

Summit of El Teide

see the gory results of Teide's most recent eruption, when in 1798 Las Narices del Teide (Teide's Nostrils) contributed their own rocky spew to these ashen badlands.

From here the descent to the coast is a welcome return to life. **La Gomera** appears on the horizon, pine trees peep through the clouds, wildflowers and cacti emerge from the rocks. This is a long and peaceful road, which is virtually unpopulated until you come to Chio. Just before the village pull over at the **Restaurante Las Estrellas**, for a reviving drink as well as the chance to savour its fine views over the coast below.

At Chio, turn left onto the C822 heading towards **Guía de Isora**. This is a much busier road and comes as something of a shock after the lulling tranquillity of Teide, so take care as it whisks you back to the bustling fury of Playa de las Américas and the coast.

Above: mountain viewpoint
Right: prickly pears

2. From Teide down to Puerto de la Cruz via the Carretera Dorsal

Return to the junction at El Portillo, this time turning right onto the high mountain road (C824) that runs along the dorsal ridge towards **La Laguna**. Built by the military in the 1940s, this is one of the most enjoyable drives in Tenerife, a pleasant descent through pine forests to the undulating farmlands of **La Esperanza,** with stunning views over both sides of the island. Unfortunately, in winter it can sometimes be blocked by snow and at other times clouds can spoil the fun.

The first sight to catch your eye is the gleaming white buildings of the **Observatorio Astronómico del Teide**, perched on **Montaña Izaña** to your right. The Observatory was originally built in 1965 to study the night sky but the bright lights generated by the tourist boom have now made this impossible. Stellar observation has been transferred to La Palma where the light is protected and the Observatorio is now used for solar studies.

As you descend from the mountainside into cool forests of eucalyptus and pine you will encounter several *miradores* whose panoramic views will make you want to stop the car and get out. The short detour out to **Mirador de las Cumbres** offers views up and down the north coast and is soon followed by more viewpoints over the island's southern slopes. Further on **Mirador Pico de las Flores** has extensive views north to La Esperanza, Santa Cruz and the Macizo de Anaga.

A short diversion then takes you deep into the tall pines of the **Bosque de la Esperanza**. Turn right at a sign to **Las Raíces** (the Roots). The road leads down to an obelisk commemorating a clandestine meeting held here by Franco and the officers of the Tenerife garrison prior to the uprising that sparked the Spanish Civil War. Today this point is an ideal starting point for a peaceful walk in the woods.

Return to the C824, continuing down to the gentle fields of **La Esperanza**. Large restaurants line the road, packed at weekends with Santacruceros who like to drive out for a long lunch followed

by a walk in the woods. On Sundays the smell of roast meat garnished with garlic and rosemary often proves irresistible: if you like the lively atmosphere of the big family lunch come around 2pm – **El Gran Chaparral** and **Las Rosas** are two of the most popular.

La Esperanza is a long, strung-out town – look out for a small turning left to Agua García (TF3118), which takes you down rural lanes walled with high hedges reminiscent of Devon or northern Spain. This road leads down to the *autopista* where you can head west to **Puerto de la Cruz**.

Franco's obelisk, Las Raíces

MACIZO DE TENO

The north-west corner of Tenerife is dominated by some of the island's oldest rock formations, stubborn basaltic lava-flows patiently sculpted by erosion to form a spectacular peninsula known as the Macizo de Teno. It's a landscape of both drama and tranquility: the northern coast is bordered by gentle volcanic plains while in the south jagged mountain ridges saw-tooth into the sea. If you want a closer view of these precipitous cliffs, called the **Acantilado de los Gigantes,** you can take a boat trip from **Los Gigantes**.

Driving round **Teno** is slow but rewarding: the roads are a raucous concertina of bends and hairpins but most have been newly surfaced. Again, you have a choice of routes: one starting from Playa de las Américas, the other from Puerto de la Cruz.

1. From Playa de las Américas

Take the main road north (C822) before turning left onto the coastal road (TF6237) towards **San Juan**. This route reveals the scale of the building boom that has recently transformed the island's

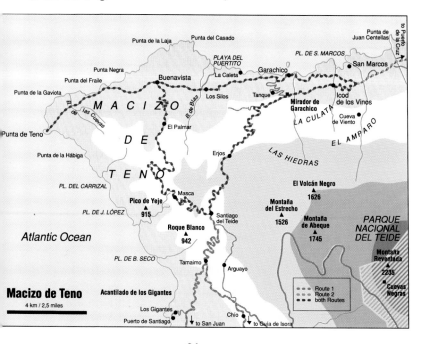

western shore. Here the *barrancos* and banana plantations are fast disappearing as the tourist complexes sweep north. San Juan may be a good example of a tiny fishing port now heading for the big time but the restaurants just up from its clear-watered harbour are well worth returning to for a typical Canary fish lunch.

Continue north as the road bypasses Puerto de Santiago, Playa de la Arena and Los Gigantes to climb towards Tamaimo (TF6281). Here the slopes are still shelved with terraces growing vines, potatoes and tomatoes – originally this was a slip-road built to take such produce down to meet the fruit-boats that regularly circled the island. Turn left at Tamaimo onto the C820 and wind your way up to the small village of **Santiago del Teide**. (For the rest of the itinerary, see *Exploring the Macizo de Teno*, below.)

2. From Puerto de la Cruz

Head west on the C820 following the signs to **Icod**. Scored out of the cliffs and dotted with tunnels, the road reveals the steeply sloping coast that characterises Tenerife's northern shore. *'Se vende vino'* signs remind you this is one of the island's oldest wine-growing areas. Pass through the outskirts of **Icod de los Vinos** (see Option 9), turning left for El Tanque by a Shell garage.

Still on the C820 (the original road linking the whole of the north) enjoy the corkscrew climb past vineyards and *lagares* (wine presses) to the **Mirador de Garachico**. Mist sometimes blots out this dramatic viewpoint but on a clear day it gives a fascinating aerial picture of the lava-swamped town of **Garachico**, virtually destroyed by an eruption of El Volcán Negro in 1706.

Continue west through El Tanque, beyond which the landscape takes on a new pastoral mood with a patchwork of small fields draped between the mountains. A sign at **Puerto de Erjos** (3,664ft, 1,117m) marks the traditional mountain pass leading to the south coast. From here it's a gentle descent into the relaxed village of **Santiago del Teide**.

EXPLORING THE MACIZO DE TENO

It is worth stopping at **Santiago del Teide**, if only for a quick drink and the chance to savour the village's easy-going atmosphere. Look inside its tiny white church, which has an attractive domed roof and an altar decorated with local flowers, fruit and embroidered linen.

Santiago del Teide Church

The smell of wax candles and the sound of taped choral song add to the inner calm of this charming church.

Just across from the church a narrow road (TF1427) leads towards **Masca**. It rises to a ridge where a small pull-in allows you to stop and absorb the views. Ahead lie the sharp peaks and valleys of the Teno massif and beyond them the island of **La Gomera**. Looking back you can see **Pico de Teide** and the slightly lower **Pico Viejo**. Nearer still you can trace the route taken by the lava-flows following the eruption of **Montaña de Chinyero** in 1909, Tenerife's most recent eruption. For 10 days it sent ash and cinders into the sky with a roar that could be heard in Orotava. Stones flew up to 2,000ft (610m) and a stream of lava (still visible through the pine trees) rolled towards Santiago del Teide at 2ft (61cm) per minute. Fortunately, the lava divided around Montaña Bilma, but it left a trail of volcanic debris three miles long by half a mile wide (4.8km by 0.8km).

Here you start the precarious descent into the **Masca Valley,** a journey that until the mid-70s was only possible by mule or on foot. As you wind your way down, look for the stone houses of Masca village way below with their

tiny vegetable plots and terraces chiselled out of the mountainside. Soon you'll spy palms and fruit trees on the valley floor, hear the tinkle of streams and pass well-loved gardens apoplectic with

Masca valley

bougainvillea. Now you can sense what an extraordinary Shangri-la this hidden valley must have been in the centuries before the modern world poked its nose over the mountains.

At the bottom there are two places to park and visit **Masca,** a village that appears caught between two ridges. From one (by the first bus stop you come to) a steep path leads down past tiny cottages – the most authentic part of the village – to a *Museo* containing a miscellany of things Mascan (currently closed for restoration). From here it's a pleasant level walk round to Masca's other half.

A second park (by the second bus stop) offers a gentle descent past the village church to several terrace restaurants. At **Casa Enrique** and **El Guanche** you can sample Mascan cuisine for around 1,200 pesetas. Specialities here include *puchero* – a vegetable soup you can thicken with *gofio,* fried goat's cheese, and *bananas creme* sweetened with date palm rum. Both restaurants are firmly on the tourist trail and can get unfittingly busy for such a peaceful valley, but they do offer interesting Canarian dishes and if you're vegetarian they're a rare find. Further along the road at **La Vica** another restaurant, **La Pimentera da Salvadores,** offers Canarian food and has probably the best views of the Masca Valley.

The ascent out of the Masca valley towards **El Palmar** is a pleasant drive with views back over the craggy mountains. In winter, wildflowers illuminate the roadside as you progress from Teno's harsh peaks down towards the gentle volcanic plains of the north coast. Finally you cross a last ridge and the open fields of El Palmar span out below. A huge cone of burnt red volcanic scoria dominates this town, out of which giant slices have been quarried to make the neighbouring houses.

From here a better road (TF 1426) takes you quickly down to **Buenavista**. On the outskirts the **Restaurante El Marino** on your left is a good point to pick up a cold drink or *bocadillo* (sandwich) before heading out to **Punta de Teno**. The road leading west to

Punta de Teno lighthouse

the lighthouses is well signposted (TF1429), passing through banana plantations and around the cliffs. Here you get a chance for a close look at the petrified violence behind Teno's immense rock formations, an angry contrast to the shimmering placidity of the Atlantic.

Garachico

The road ends at a flat expanse where sun and sea magnify the rich colours of the lava – a debris of ochres, reds and blacks where a luminous euphorbia struggles to gain hold. There's not much of a beach here, but a small fishermen's quay allows for a swim off the rocks. You can also walk out to two lonely lighthouses, or just sit and watch the clouds nudging **La Gomera**.

From here you must return along the same road to Buenavista, then continue straight on east through the cobbled streets of Los Silos. Carry along the TF142 to **Garachico,** one of Tenerife's best preserved towns – if you've made good progress it's ideal for a late afternoon stroll (see *Option 10, page 72*). To return home, follow one of the next two routes.

1. From Garachico to Playa de las Américas

On the western edge of Garachico a steep switchback road (TF1421) loops up the mountainside to the Mirador de Garachico. For a gentler ascent continue on through Garachico to Icod de los Vinos (see Option 9), turning right at a Shell garage for El Tanque (C820). This road winds up through terraces of vines to the **Mirador de Garachico,** where there's a bar (inevitably) and panoramic views over the lava-flows that swamped Garachico in 1706.

Carry along the C820 past El Tanque and through the mountain pass of **Puerto de Erjos** (3,664ft, 1,117m). From here decorative lines of cacti pot-plants begin to appear on rooftops, and small cultivated plateaux growing cabbages and potatoes signify the start of your descent to the warm south. Pass through Santiago del Teide and continue along the high road (C820) towards **Guía de Isora**. From here the road (C822) cuts across the deep *barrancos* serrating the land, past huge pens of Triffid-like bananas and back down to **Playa de las Américas**.

2. From Garachico to Puerto de la Cruz

Continue east to Icod where you rejoin the C820. This takes you back to **Puerto de la Cruz.**

Anaga mountains

THE ANAGA MOUNTAINS

Rising out of the ocean like the jagged spine of a prehistoric monster, the **Anaga mountains** fill Tenerife's northeastern corner. Like the Macizo de Teno they are some of the island's oldest rocks, razor-edged peaks that must have formed a forbidding backdrop for the *conquistadores* who founded their first settlement on the uplands of La Laguna. Even today their saw-toothed silhouette provides a sharp riposte to the pretentious skyline of the island's modern capital, Santa Cruz.

The **Macizo** (Massif) del Anaga is one of Tenerife's most spectacular landscapes, a savage scenery that conceals some of the island's most peaceful spots. Only some parts are accessible by road and its remotest valleys still cradle isolated farming communities that until recently dwelt in mountain caves untainted by electricity. It's best to make an early start so you can enjoy Anaga at a leisurely pace — the roads here are slow and serpentine, sometimes perilous. They're gradually being resurfaced but remain prone to mist and blockage from snow or rockfalls. Before setting off fill up with petrol.

If you don't fancy the driving you could take a taxi tour or one of the TITSA buses that serve its far-flung points (see *Getting Around*). Anaga is also a paradise for the experienced and well-organised walker (see *Walking*).

There is a choice of routes, depending on your starting point.

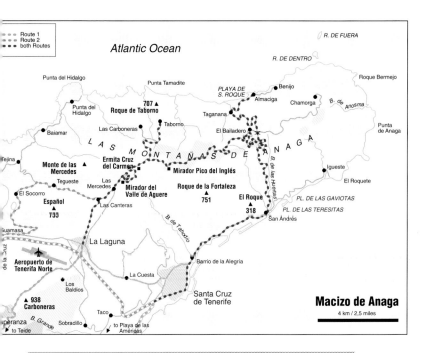

1. From Playa de las Américas

As the Anaga mountains lie at the opposite end of the island your day will involve more driving than in other itineraries. If you prefer to keep this to a minimum it's an easy journey to and from La Laguna by *autopista*. To get there take this east towards Santa Cruz (TF1), turning off before you enter the city onto the Autopista del Norte (TF5). This takes you to La Laguna. A good stop along this route would be a visit to the basilica at **Candelaria** (see Option 13).

For a longer scenic drive (early start essential) take the *autopista* east (TF1) as far as the Güimar exit. Turn off here, taking the road up through Güimar (TF612) and then following the signs to **Arafo** (TF4132). This is a quiet and pretty hillside town overlooking the fertile Güimar valley. The small bars around its central square, **Plaza de José Antonio** are a convenient place to break your journey.

From Arafo you begin a steep and enjoyable climb up to the island's dorsal ridge, with good views back to the coast. The road winds up into the pines to join the mountain-top road near Mirador Ortuño, where you turn right (C824). If the clouds permit, you will have fine vistas of the north coast as you drop gently through the fragrant pine forests. Be sure to stop at **Mirador Pico de las Flores,** from where you can see the Anaga mountains patiently awaiting your visit. Continue your descent through the woods and fields of La Esperanza to the historic town of La Laguna.

La Laguna's grid of Renaissance streets (see Option 7) were not designed for modern-day traffic but if you follow the signs to **Las Mercedes** that thread through the city you'll emerge in a pleasant avenue lined with eucalyptus trees (TF121). This takes you up to **Las Canteras,** where you turn right (TF114), curving up into laurel forest and the **Mirador del Valle de Aguere** (for the rest of this journey, see *Exploring the Anaga Mountains,* below).

2. From Puerto de la Cruz

Leave Puerto de la Cruz by the *autopista,* heading east towards Santa Cruz (TF5). Turn off at the Guamasa exit, following signs towards the town but turning right after the bridge onto the old road (C820) that runs parallel with the *autopista.* Continue east to a turn-off left for Tegueste (TF 1213). This road trickles down through a well-tended terraced valley as yet unmarred by *urbanización.* Pass through El Socorro to Tegueste, turning right here (TF 121) as the road climbs past ancient Canary pines to Las Canteras. Here you turn a hard left (by Bar Alonso) following signs to **Monte de las Mercedes** (TF114). The road climbs steadily into the laurel forest and the **Mirador del Valle de Aguere.**

EXPLORING THE ANAGA MOUNTAINS

Perched on Monte de las Mercedes, the **Mirador del Valle de Aguere** offers your first chance to look back over the verdant plateau upon which La Laguna rests. Behind this you can see Tenerife's dorsal ridge rising towards Teide's peak. From here the road (TF114) continues further up into the thick, evergreen laurel forest that originally covered most of Tenerife's northern slopes. Soon you come to another viewpoint, **Mirador Cruz del Carmen,** with good views over this sylvan scene. A small early 17th-century chapel nearby pays homage to Nuestra Señora de las Mercedes.

Continue on the TF114, bearing right at the next junction to follow the signs to **Mirador del Pico del Inglés.** This side road leads out to a mountain-top promontory known as The Englishman's Peak (3,149ft, 960m), so-called because of an Englishman, who is said to have walked from La Laguna to here in a day. The road ends in a loop where you can park and walk out to a viewing plat-

form. With so many *miradores,* Tenerife sometimes seems an appallingly vain and self-admiring island but you will find this vantage point definitely panoramic. It gives some of the best views over the island, allowing you to contrast the ancient zig-zag of the

Taborno

Anaga's peaks and valleys with the proud, uneroded cone of Teide.

Drive back to the junction where you turned off for Pico del Inglés. Resume your original journey by turning right – you are now following the signs to **Las Carboneras.** Soon you will come to another junction where you turn left, signposted to Las Carboneras and Taborno. (If you have come from Playa de las Américas you may prefer to omit this detour (45min) and proceed straight to **Taganana** for a well-deserved lunch. To do this turn right instead (TF1123), signposted to El Bailadero and pick up the itinerary again two paragraphs below.)

The road to Las Carboneras (TF1145) curls dramatically down the northern slopes of Anaga offering glimpses through the laurel forest to a solitary peak, **Roque de Taborno.** Soon you will have an opportunity to pull in and absorb the views. Beneath you the mountains cascade towards the sea, sprinkled with the tiny white houses of two isolated villages – Las Carboneras (The Charcoal Burners) and, caught on a knife-blade of rock, Taborno.

Continue your descent, in due course turning right for Taborno (TF1128). The road leads to the end of the ridge with views across the valley to Las Carboneras, finally coming to rest at the small school, *ermita* and plaza that are **Taborno.** Here, as you'll find at the end of every Spanish road, there is a bar. It's an ideal place to pause and enjoy the peace concealed in Anaga's rugged folds. Plummeting ravines fall away to either side of the village while ahead rises the toothy rock of Taborno, long revered by the Guanches and still charismatic. As you watch the straw-hatted workers tilling their terraces way below it's not hard to imagine what life must have been like in the long centuries before the road – only recently completed – came over the mountain.

This road is also the only way you'll get back to the modern world and the chance of a decent lunch. Head back up the valley, rejoining the TF1145 and climbing to the junction with the main

TF1123. Turn left towards El Bailadero, an exhilarating drive that rides the Anaga's ridges, weaving either side of mountain-tops and giving a good view of the Macizo's southern slopes. Follow the signs to Taganana – you'll have to turn right (TF1112), apparently in the wrong direction – dropping down towards San Andrés but then doubling back (turn left onto the TF1134) through a mountain tunnel that brings you out on the northern coast. From here you make a sweeping descent to the sea on a looping road embroidered onto the mountainside. Far below you lies the village of **Taganana,** which you will eventually reach.

Continue past Taganana until you are down by the sea. Soon you will encounter a string of roadside restaurants facing a small beach, **Playa del Roque.** This is a fine place for a late lunch—unsophisticated, popular, typically Canarian. Most of these restaurants have no name, hardly any have menus, but what they do have is fish, always served in the Canary way with *papas arrugadas* and *mojo* sauce and accompanied by a mixed salad blessed with delicious avocado. Have nothing less, and wash it down with some local *vino rosado*. And all for around 3,000ptas for two.

When suitably refreshed, make the ascent back through Taganana and up into the mountains. Pass through the tunnel again, continuing straight on down towards the southern coast (TF112). Now you make the descent down the island's drier side, its hills speckled with remote *fincas,* the valley floors a haven for vegetable plots and fruit trees. In time the road winds down to the fishing village of San Andrés and to its north (turn left) the sandy smile of **Playa de las Teresitas**. After your epic drive up and down the Macizo de Anaga the only way to celebrate your safe return to sea-level is with a relaxing swim on this well-kept beach, or a least a cold drink in one of its shady kiosks. To return to your starting point, take one of the following routes.

1. From San Andrés to Playa de las Américas

Take the TF111 south into Santa Cruz. Unless you plan to stop here (see Option 1), follow the coastal road around the city, past Plaza de España and up the multi-laned Avenida Tres de Mayo. Bear left to join the Autopista del Sur (TF1), which will take you back to Playa de las Américas.

2. From San Andrés to Puerto de la Cruz

From San Andrés take the TF111 south towards Santa Cruz. Unless you plan to visit the city (see Option 1), continue along the seafront as far as the Club Náutico, then turn right up the Rambla del General Franco. This joins up with the multi-laned Avenida Tres de Mayo. Bear right for the Autopista del Norte (TF5) which takes you back past La Laguna and on to Puerto de la Cruz.

Santa Cruz

A few years ago most visitors to Santa Cruz found the island's capital a chaotic and polluted place, its streets molested by traffic, the seafront disfigured by the ugly architecture major international ports inevitably spawn. Today, like many other Spanish cities, it is taking a new pride in its appearance. Though it remains at heart an old-fashioned jumble of small shops and narrow streets, its seafront promenade has at last been spruced up and a walk down Avenida de Anaga with its tropical palms and colourful oleander bushes is an agreeable experience, especially when the port is busy with ferries and cruise liners.

As capital of the western province of the Canary Islands Santa Cruz leads a busy administrative life and – unlike many parts of Tenerife – makes few concessions to the demands of mass tourism. Instead it exists for its own citizens, the Santacruceros. They're a spirited and friendly bunch, and every year they hold the second largest carnival in the world to prove it (See *Special Events, page 96*).

If you're planning a trip to Santa Cruz consider using the express bus service *(directo)* – line 111 from Playa de las Américas (90 min), 102 from Puerto de la Cruz (60 min). Try to get there by 11am and don't forget to take your swimming costume.

Above: All tooled up
Left: Civil War Memorial
Right: Plaza de Candelaria, 187

1. Santa Cruz City-Centre Walk (half day)

This tour starts at the city's hub, the **Plaza de España.** If you're driving here the carpark on the seafront side of the square is your best bet. If you arrive by bus, cross the broad Avenida Tres de Mayo and walk down Calle de José Hernández Alonso to the central market. Pick up the tour from there, carrying on round from Plaza de España at the end (see map).

In the centre of Plaza de España stands the grim **Monumento de los Caídos,** a memorial to those who fell in the Spanish Civil War. Two suppliant Guanche chieftains stand in front, their bowed heads behatted with pigeons. To the north the peaks of the Anaga mountains mock the city's high-rise buildings, suitably unimpressed by the Francoist pomp of the towering **Palacio Insular** that dominates the Plaza's southwestern corner. This is the seat of the island's **Cabildo** or government – inside the main foyer there's an interesting large scale relief model of Tenerife, while next door is the Tourist Information Office (open 8am–3pm Monday to Saturday, closes at 2pm in summer, 9am–1pm Saturday).

A second pedestrianised square, the **Plaza de Candelaria,** joins onto Plaza de España. As plazas go it's surprisingly useful, and a lot of visitors never seem to get far beyond it. If you need some fortification first, a coffee on the terrace of the nearby **Bar Olimpo** is a popular solution, while the comfortable chairs of the **Bar Atlántico** opposite are an ideal place to meet up with your companions after shopping.

At one end of the Plaza stands a marble statue by Canova depicting the *Triunfo de la Candelaria,* erected in 1778. This celebrates the Virgin of Candelaria, patroness of the whole Canary Islands archipelago. She is typically shown holding a naked infant in her right arm and a candle in the other, with four Guanche *menceys* paying homage below (see *Option 13, page 75*).

Just up from this statue at No. 9 is the former Palacio de Carta, now the **Banco Español de Crédito.** This is the place to change some money, a traditional Canarian mansion dating from 1774 with carved wooden balconies and a plant-filled patio that must

Plaza de la Iglesia

make it one of the world's most elegant *bureaux de change*. A few doors up is **Artespaña,** part of a state-owned chain of shops selling Spanish arts and crafts. Prices here are fair, with Canarian goods well represented – along with costumed dolls, embroidered linen and the omnipresent *Lladro*, you can also buy rarer items, like banana leaf baskets, Gomeran pottery and traditional outfits as worn by the *campesinos* of La Palma.

The opposite side of the Plaza leads into **Calle del Castillo,** Santa Cruz's main shopping drag. Two useful shops are the department store **Maya** (just off the Plaza) which encapsulates in one building most of what you'll find on offer everywhere else; back towards the statue, **La Casa de los Balcones** is a small branch of the embroidery school in La Orotava (see *Option 8, page 69*).

Walk back down from Plaza de Candelaria, turning right by the Caja Postal into Avenida Bravo Murillo, where you pass the Museo Arqueológico (see Option 2 below). This takes you into the charming **Plaza de la Iglesia** where 19th-century buildings pay their respects to the Iglesia Nuestra Señora de la Concepción. Look out for the Tinerfeña building (1880), testimony to the days when the tobacco trade brought wealth to some islanders.

The Iglesia's six-tier belfry is one of Santa Cruz's most famous landmarks. The church was built in 1502 but the present structure is largely the result of renovation during the 17th and 18th centuries. It is currently closed for more restoration. The nave has long been a depository for the city's historic treasures, including the *Cruz de la Conquista* (Cross of the Conquest) planted by De Lugo on his landing in 1496 (from which the city received its name) and the flags won following Nelson's abortive attack on the port in 1797 – now housed in the **Museo Militar** (the Regional Military Museum – see Option 2 below).

It's a short walk from the entrance to the church to the **Barranco de Santos,** a deep gully and old city boundary. Turn right to walk alongside it, opposite the old Civil Hospital which houses the **Museo Insular de Ciencas Naturales** (Museum of Natural Science), until a small bridge takes you through Calle Quinta to the city's main market, Nuestra Señora de África (open Monday–Saturday until 1pm). A grand arch packed with flower sellers leads into the arcaded *mercado,* crowned with an apricot bell-tower. This is a good opportunity to pick up some fresh fruit or local delicacies. Downstairs on your right a small stall sells produce brought

over from the tiny island of El Hierro – try some of their cheese made from a blend of cow, goat and sheep milk and known as *queso herreño,* either *ahumada* (smoked) or *curada* (mature). The stall also sells local wine, honey and pineapples. Outside, more stalls pile the pavements with a madness of wares. Around the entrance is a good place to pick up some Canarian or Latin American music – look out for cassettes by local *orquestas* from around 600ptas.

Along **Calle José Manuel Guimerá** traders sell a jumble of kitchen utensils, clothes and religious knickknacks. Beach shoes, straw hats and leather goods are some of the

The arcaded market

Parque Municipal García Sanabria

best buys. From the main entrance to the market, walk straight ahead across Puente Serrador. This passes through what was the the old, poor side of Santa Cruz (fast being knocked down) back to the pedestrianised shopping street **Calle del Castillo.** Turn left and walk up towards **Plaza de Weyler.** A sticky cake from **Pastelería Claribel** (No. 59) or an *helado* (ice-cream) from **La Gelatería Italiana** will help keep the crowds at bay.

Plaza de Weyler and its neighbouring streets contain Santa Cruz's grandest buildings, most of which are now banks and administrative headquarters. Bear right at the top down Calle Méndez Nuñez, past the *Ayuntiamento* (Town Hall) and into the **Parque Municipal García Sanabria.** This is a typically Spanish, typically civic park with old men, tiled benches, newspaper and refreshment kiosks and dusty gravel paths. It dates from the 1920s, although the presence of several uncollected works left over from an international sculpture exhibition held in 1973 do bring it slightly nearer the modern world.

Leave the park near the floral clock, heading down Calle Pilar past the Iglesia del Pilar. At the bottom lies the department stores **El Cortes Inglés** and **Galerías Preciados,** which conveniently stay open throughout the afternoon. On the far side of the Plaza del Patriotismo is the Calle de la Rosa and, at its opposite end, the Museo Militar, or Military Museum (see Option 2 below).

For lunch the **Plaza del Príncipe de Asturias** at the bottom of Calle del Pilar is a shady oasis that still retains the genteel atmosphere that must have once pervaded all Santa Cruz once upon a time. Originally the garden of a Franciscan friary, the Plaza del Príncipe is graced by the pleasant **Café El Príncipe** (Tel: 27 88 10). Stop for a drink, *tapas* or some *'cocina canaria y nuevas creacions,'* all served alfresco. Here you can have lunch the way the Santacruceros like it: simple food, well cooked – perhaps some *sopa de pescado* or *conejo en salmorejo* (rabbit in spicy sauce). Characteristically, there are no concessions made for tourists (no translations, no flags, no credit cards). Expect to pay around 4,000ptas for two.

From here you can walk down from the Plaza, past the 17th century **Iglesia de San Francisco,** formerly a chapel founded by Irish Catholics fleeing the persecution of Elizabeth I, and into Calle de Béthencourt Alfonso. This will lead you back to Plaza de España. Now you can do what all Santacruceros do once the shops and offices have closed for the afternoon – head for the beach.

Five miles (eight km) to the north lies one of the island's best beaches, **Las Teresitas.** You can drive or take bus 10 to San Andrés from Avenida Anaga. Near to where it stops you'll see the circular walls of the **Castillo de San Andrés** (built 1706-41), which have now split in two like a broken cup. Las Teresitas lies before you, a vast man-made beach constructed in the 1970s with sand imported from the Spanish Sahara. A long breakwater of boulders ensures it stays there, and guarantees the water's safe for all to swim.

2. Santa Cruz Museums (one hour each)

If you're interested in Tenerife's history, two of Santa Cruz's museums are well worth a visit. Both are small, thought-provoking and won't tire your feet.

Museo Arqueológico, Avenida Bravo Murillo (Open 9am–1pm and 4–6pm Monday to Friday, 9am–1pm Saturday.) Just round the corner from the Tourist Office, the Archaelogical Museum (Avenida Bravo Murillo) quietly displays an engaging collection of Guanche relics. These include tools, weapons, pottery and jewellery discovered from the days when Tenerife's aboriginal inhabitants ruled the island. They were a pastoral, patriarchal society and in certain ways quite advanced from the primitive cavemen depicted in tourist leaflets.

Like the Egyptians this mysterious race, whose origins are still the subject of debate, mummified their dead, stuffing the corpses with animal fat and wrapping them in hide. These would be buried high up in remote caves and *barrancos* where even today they're still being discovered. The *Museo* has many such finds, including wizened full-size skeletons and – in a far room stacked with a Golgotha of skulls – evidence that the Guanches even practised a rudimentary form of surgery using sharp cutting-stones.

Museo Militar (Open Tuesday to Sunday, 10am–2pm. You may be asked to show some form of identification, such as your passport, before entering.) A ten-minute walk north from the Plaza de España is the Regional Military Museum of the Canary Islands. It's housed in the **Almeida Barracks** in **Calle San Isidro,** constructed between 1854 and 1884 in a rather playful semi-circular design, and gives an intriguing insight into Canarian military life past and present. (You may well be escorted all the time, probably by a teenager from Barcelona doing his three months' conscription duty.) Of particular interest to British visitors are the spoils of war resulting from Nelson's failed attempt to seize Santa Cruz in 1797 (see *History*). Exhibits include 'El Tigre', the cannon alleged to have shot our hero's arm off, tattered flags from *HMS Emerald* and a copy

47

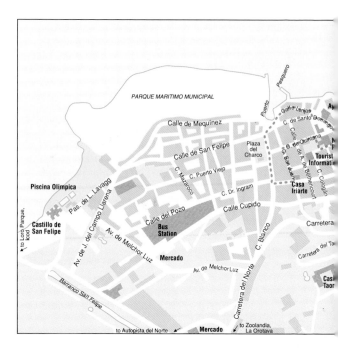

of the toadying 'thank you' letter written by Nelson to the Spanish commander after the engagement: 'I beg your Excellency will honour me with your acceptance of a cask of English beer and cheese…'

Other curiosities include weapons and armour from the *conquistadores'* defeat at La Matanza de Acentejo in 1494 and booty from the Spanish occupation of the Philippines. There's also a 'Franco corner' commemorating his four months as Comandante-General de Canarias, which includes the great dictator's desk, a photograph of his meeting with fellow-conspirators near Las Raíces and a map outlining the route of the famous 'Dragon Rapide' aeroplane that

Museo Arqueológico

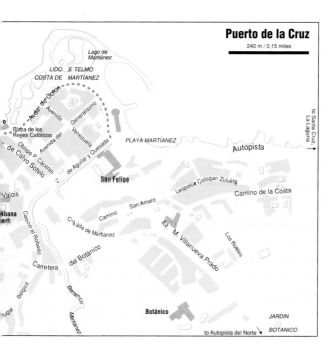

in 1936 flew from Croydon to the Canaries and thence with him
to Morocco and the start of the Spanish Civil War (see *History*).

Puerto de la Cruz

Puerto de la Cruz has a long tradition of hospitality to foreigners
and you won't have to walk far to find yourself in a *calle* incon-

grously named after a former citizen
like Ingram, Murphy, Yeoward or Col-
gan. It's a major tourist resort now,
with some 900,000 annual visitors, but
Puerto (as it's affectionately known)
still strives to greet its guests with a relaxed and courteous face, as if we'd
all just stepped off the weekly packet
from Liverpool.

Originally known as Puerto de la
Orotava, the town grew out of a small
quay which used to export the sugar
grown by Tenerife's early colonists.
After an eruption of Teide in 1706 destroyed the nearby port of Garachico
(see Option 10) it rapidly became the
island's main outlet for produce
grown in the rich Valle de la Orotava
above. Canary wine was shipped from
here for over a century, to be fol-

lowed by cochineal and bananas. From the 1880s Puerto de la Cruz began to attract tourists, particularly the British, who relished the beneficial winter climate and scenery of Orotava and resided in grand hotels that still bejewel the town.

Puerto still has a large and vocal British community with its own Games Club, Library and Anglican church up in the hills overlooking the town. Known as Parque Taoro, this is an area of exclusive residences and secluded hotels, crowned by the grand Casino Taoro (see *Nightlife*). The Parque's spacious gardens are in marked contrast to the congestion you'll encounter down by the seafront: either walk down or use the town's excellent taxi service. Much of Puerto has been blanket-bombed by characterless architecture, but nevertheless you'll find that its heart is mercifully pedestrianised and quite amiable.

3. Puerto de la Cruz Town Walk (half day)

Taxi drivers have a knack of congregating in the best parts of town and the busy rank in Plaza del Charco is a free pavement cabaret. The square is Puerto's social centre and the best way to introduce yourself is with a *café solo* in one of its many bars – the **Paraiso de Tenerife** (No. 4) is a popular choice. Before you settle down, nip across to the kiosk opposite and buy a copy of *The Island Sun*, a local English language paper that will give you all the news in the islands.

Properly known as **Plaza del Charco de los Camarones** (The Square of the Shrimp Pool), the area used to fill up at high tide when the locals would turn out to catch shrimps. Its huge Indian laurel trees were imported from Cuba in 1852, and have provided shade for countless games of cards and chess and regularly given support to the bright lights of *carnaval*.

From the plaza's northwest corner a short street leads seawards, Calle de María. This will take you to the old **Puerto Pesquero,** bright with joyfully-painted fishing boats that still return early in the morning with the daily catch – although you'll not see much activity there during the rest of the day. The harbour is the focus of Puerto's annual *fiesta* in honour of the Virgen del Carmen, that includes the nocturnal burning of a giant mock sardine full of fireworks (see *Calendar of Special Events, page 96*).

On the east side of the harbour stands the large white and stone **Casa de la Real Aduana,** Puerto's oldest surviving building. Dating from 1620, it served as the Royal Customs House until 1833. Follow the cobbled Calle las

Fiesta in Puerto Pesquero

Casa de la Real Aduana

Lonjas, which curves round past the modern *Ayuntiamento* (Town Hall) with the early 18th-century **Casa Miranda** opposite. This was originally the family home of Francisco de Miranda, a local hero who played a leading role in Venezuela's long struggle for independence. Today Casa Miranda is an elegant restaurant with a bar and coffee shop downstairs.

Soon you will reach a terrace with a fine view along the coast and the waves crashing against the rocky shore below. This point is known locally as **Punta del Viento** on account of the head-on winds you can no doubt feel. Continue on down the steps and along the pedestrianised shopping promenade, Calle de San Telmo. To your left another flight of steps leads down to sea-water swimming pools and a bar where you can sit and watch the local children brave the rolling waves.

The *paseo* carries on up into Avenida de Colón, passing the small white **Capilla San Telmo.** Built in 1626, repeatedly restored through the centuries and now surrounded by a circus of tourist activity, it still retains the simple piety of a fishermen's chapel. It is dedicated to San Telmo (St Elmo), an Italian bishop who had his intestines wound around a windlass in the 4th century. A traditional patron saint of sailors (and also stomach disorders), his name is sometimes used to describe the blue stormlights on ships,

Puerto Pesquero

known as St Elmo's fire. Close to the chapel is the **Plaza de los Reyes Católicos,** containing a bust of Francisco de Miranda. From here **Avenida de Colón** curls round the shore, a busy avenue lined on one side with stalls selling crafts, clothes and jewellery. Beyond these lies the magnificent Lago de Martiánez complex, a series of artificial swimming pools well worth returning to later on during your stay. The Avenida ends inconsequentially at the Hotel San Felipe and a small beach frequented by ambitious anglers. This is the point from which many of the free excursion buses depart (*see Option 4 page 54*).

Buy yourself an ice cream and head back along the promenade, doing your best to avoid the timeshare touts and parrot-shouldered photographers. Soon after you pass the Capilla San Telmo turn left down a small alley that takes you into Calle de la Hoya, where you walk right. This takes you down a thoroughly modern street packed with British bars and pubs. If you fancy a game of pool and a pint of proper English bitter stop now. If not, continue straight on until you reach the calm of the **Plaza de la Iglesia.** Have a seat...

Café Columbus Beach

In front of you on the square rises Puerto's main church, **Nuestra Señora de la Peña de Francia,** surrounded by towering palm trees. Begun in 1697, it has been consistently re-structured by Puerto's citizens ever since. The organ comes from London, installed in 1814 by a resident of Irish descent, Bernardo de Cologán.

To the right of the church the shop Trebol specialises in Canarian hand-embroidered cloth *manteleria* (table linen). This is the type of fixed-price shop to visit if you want to buy genuine local crafts – most street-sellers sell imports from China.

In the plaza is a statue commemorating the engineer Augustín de Bethancourt who was born in Puerto de la Cruz in 1798. He rose to become a general in the Russian army and built roads, bridges and canals for Tsar Alexander I.

The Plaza also has the **Tourist Information Office** (open 9am–8pm Monday to Friday, 9am–1pm Saturday). Down one side runs Calle de Quintana, dominated by two of Puerto's oldest hotels, the **Monopol** (1742) and the **Marquesa** (1712). Both have been drastically renovated, but their Canary balconies and patios still give an idea of the turn-of-the-century elegance they offered Puerto's first tourists, who came to the Canary Islands to experience the beneficial climate. The terrace of the Marquesa is a pleasant place to sit and watch plaza life, particularly in the early evening as people *paseo* before dinner.

Walk down Calle Quintana, turning left into Calle San Juan. This street has many shops selling threadwork, embroidery and traditional Canarian crafts, as well as a small department store **Gómez Baeza** (No. 10). **Casa Iriarte** at the end of the street is another fine 18th-century building, its beauty masked by a clutter of souvenirs on sale. On its top floor is a dishevelled **Naval Museum** with a motley display of model ships, scrimshaw and nautical curiosities, best saved for a rainy day – if you are unfortunate enough to experience one.

Turn right here into Calle Iriarte and then right again down Calle Blanco. On the way you will pass the Restaurante La Caudra (No. 9), a pavement restaurant popular with both tourists and Canarians.

Calle Blanco returns you to Plaza del Charco and the welcome prospect of lunch. Here you have several choices, all of them pretty good. **Rincón del Puerto** on the far side (no. 14) is an old Canarian building dating from 1739 with wooden balconies and a *patio* that has been converted into six restaurants and two bars. All of these offer a range of Canarian and international food with **Restaurante Mario** specialising in fish, or you can just have a beer and some *tapas* at **Bar Olympia**. If these are packed out, **La Casona** next door is its modern equivalent with restful fountains, taped music and soporific chairs. Try its kebabs of mixed meat or fish, or cook your own steak on a slab of red-hot volcanic stone (around 4,000ptas for two). Alternatively, Calle San Felipe leads off from the taxi rank to an area of old fishermen's houses with plenty more restaurants – **La Chimenea** and **La Roda Gallega** in this street are recommended.

Canarian Crafts

Dotted in and around Puerto de la Cruz you will find a good range of attractions perfect for an easy-going morning or idle afternoon. Many of them suitable for children, and some operate their own well-publicised, free transport. Those that don't can easily be reached by taxi.

Top of your list should be the **Lago de Martiánez** complex (often called 'The Lido'), a series of eight swimming pools built on

Lago de Martiánez

reclaimed land beside Avenida Colón. Designed by the Lanzarotean artist César Manrique in 1977, it skilfully absorbs hundreds of bathers without ever seeming crowded. Decorative plants and palms border its bright blue pools while fountains, lava islands and giant sculptures entertain the swimmers. Wait for a sunny day (if you can) – admission is 335ptas and you can hire beds and sun umbrellas to really make a day of it.

The Lago also has a good range of food and drink venues, offering everything from simple hamburgers and sandwiches to a full-blown four-course meal; the complex even has a subterranean nightclub called **Andromeda** with a restaurant and nightly floorshow, open 9pm–3am.

Another must is the famous **Jardín Botánico**, just by the Carretera del Botánico (open daily 9am–7pm, admission 100ptas). Before you go, buy a bag of *fresas* (strawberries) or *cerezas* (cherries) and take all your unwritten postcards: the garden is a refreshing, relaxing haven in which to unwind, especially on hot days.

Founded in 1788 by order of Carlos III, its full title, El Jardín de Aclimatación de la Orotava, reflects its original purpose as a halfway house in which tropical plants brought from the Spanish colonies could be acclimatised prior to their introduction to mainland Spain. This followed the failure of similar schemes set up in the Royal Gardens in Madrid and Aranjuez – unfortunately, few plants made a successful transfer from Tenerife either. However, many did take root in these Botanical Gardens, so much so that its 5 acres (2 hectares) has become a fantastic jungle bursting with some 4,000 exotic plants, many of which have now reached monster proportions. The garden's centrepiece is an amazing giant South

American rubber tree (*coussapa dealbata*), thought to be two centuries old.

Up in Parque Taora, the gardens of the **Tigaiga Hotel** allow you to meet similar tropical plants in a more leisurely setting (admission 275ptas). This is a quiet, refined hotel that has recently been refurbished to a high standard. On Sunday mornings it stages displays of local folk-dancing and Canary wrestling. For further information on these events, telephone 38 35 00.

Puerto also caters for other horticultural interests with the **Rosaleda** rose gardens in nearby **La Paz** (open 9am–5pm, a free bus is available from the seafront near Hotel San Felipe).

Another popular excursion is to the **Loro Parque** in the Punta Brava district to the west of Puerto de la Cruz. Parrots are the main attraction here – the park claims to have the world's largest collection of these flying extroverts (around 200 types) – and some fly freely around while others

Jardín Botánico

give regular performances of circus tricks. The Loro Parque is virtually a zoo set in tropical gardens and its residents include gorillas, tigers, crocodiles, turtles, flamingos and pelicans. Also here is Lorovision, a wraparound cinema, which gives a stomach-churning sense of what it's like to fly; Europe's largest dophinarium; sealion displays; and an aquarium with sharks swimming overhead. The Loro Parque complex is open 8.30am–6pm daily and again a frequent free bus service operates from the seafront near Hotel San Felipe; admission charges: adults 2,500ptas, children 1,250ptas.

For a crash course in everything there is to know about the banana, **Banarera el Guanche** is the place to head. A private plantation near La Orotava, it operates guided tours and a video show in English that reveal the extraordinary background to this hermaphroditic rhizome (which despite its size is a plant not a tree). There's also a cacti garden with some 400 varieties, a walkway through a world of exotic fruit trees ranging from mango to chewing gum (a good chance to meet the source of all those flavours that now make choosing an ice-cream such a difficult task) and other crop-yielding plants, such as tobacco, ginseng, coffee, peanuts and sugar. Open 8.30am–6.30pm daily, free bus from the seafront near Hotel San Felipe.

Playa de las Américas and Los Cristianos

Southern Tenerife has always had a wild and lawless reputation, its barren coast a regular haunt of pirates and slave-raiders. The first Spanish settlers (many of whom were criminals and fugitives themselves) colonised it cautiously, building fortified settlements in the hills that are now the small villages scattered along the south's old and twisted high road (C822).

This unruly tradition continues today, flashing cockily from the brash lights of the tourist resorts that have landed all along Tenerife's southern shores. Here the Jolly Roger Fun Cruise plies the coast, carting its victims off for sun and san-

gria. Beach-slaves lie corralled on the shore, slowly cooking on hot black sand while their masters retire to shady bars to plot post office raids in Cricklewood.

The gaudiest jewel of them all is **Playa de las Américas,** set in a parched landscape of cacti and Marlboro billboards that kindles this Wild West mood. Thirty years ago the only fast movers in this desert were lizards – now it's a playground for property developers and a tourist mecca that draws one and a quarter million holidaymakers a year. You'll either love it or hate it – you certainly won't be indifferent, for here the will to party is strident and infectious.

If it's all too much, the old fishing port of **Los Cristianos** to the south is quieter, although as the two resorts rapidly merge this is likely to change. It's a short ride there in a taxi and frequent buses travel between the two. Alternatively, you can enjoy the long seafront walk outlined below.

5: Seafront Walk (half-day)

In Playa de las Américas the only way to start your day is with a Full English Breakfast. Be sure to have one before embarking on this leisurely walk—there's hardly a *bar-restaurante* that doesn't have a board up detailing the number of eggs, sausages and rashers of bacon you can expect (but not necessarily get) for around 400ptas.

Above and Right: Playa de las Américas, developed since 1965

The walk begins at the north end of Playa de las Américas at **Puerto Colón,** a prestigious new marina and beach complex adjacent to Torviscas Playa. There is parking nearby. If you are disabled or have a pushchair you may prefer to start the walk further south by the Gran Tinerfe Hotel, after which there are no steps.

Look for a tall, circular blue and white building with a dramatic suspension bridge walkway at the top. This platform is a good place to inspect the yachts and gin palaces floating in the marina below, pleasurecraft that reflect the new up-market image Tenerife is currently keen to adopt. It also offers views northwards of the development rapidly spreading up the coast. It's hard to believe, but in 1965 Playa de las Américas didn't exist. Then there were no beaches, no water, roads or electricity, not even a banana plantation—only the wild dreams of a Catalan detergent manufacturer and a local landowner who somehow found the nerve to start building holiday hotels in the middle of a scrubby nowhere.

Next to the **Aquamarina Centro Comercial,** a pedestrian walkway leads off southwards around the coast. Take this, known locally as Geranium Walk on account of its floral borders. It passes the enormous **Hotel Jardin Tropical,** a fine example of the salt-and pepper-pot architecture imported from southern Spain. Its Las Rocas restaurant is open to the public. This area is a favourite hang-out for timeshare touts offering unbelievable gifts in exchange for two hours in their hard-sell boxing ring. Unless you're seriously interested in buying property on the island (see *Shopping, page 89*) don't waste your time. They're only interested in married couples, so just look lonely and walk straight on mumbling to yourself in Chinese.

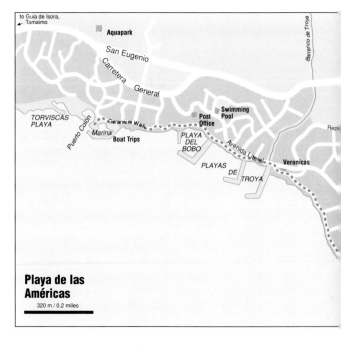

Playa de las Américas

320 m / 0,2 miles

Playa del Bobo

The walkway turns a corner dominated by bars and shops catering mainly for Germans – **Restaurante Wolfi** is a pleasant stop, with high views out to sea. All the restaurants along this walk offer identical meals geared to the international tourist, so it's really a matter of picking one with chairs that appeal to your posterior. Keep an eye out for blackboards advertising the day's speciality – such as fresh tuna with salad for 600ptas – which are always a good bet. Alternatively, you can join the army of beach bums and promenaders who survive indulgently on takeaway snacks, ice-creams and continuous beer.

Ahead you will see Playa de las Américas' three main beaches, **Playa del Bobo** and the two **Playas de Troya.** All have been artificially improved and are now cushioned with imported sand and protected by a dog-leg breakwater made of large boulders. Descend the steps to the main seafront promenade, past the Fawlty Towers Pub and the Playa de las Américas Casino (see *Nightlife*). Further on, you pass the **Acuarío Atlántico,** a seawater aquarium with huge tanks where you can meet some of the bright and brutish characters found in the waters off the Canary Islands. The collection includes baby sharks, manta rays, sea turtles, moray eels and that tasty whopper

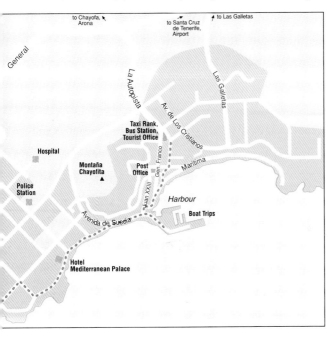

the *mero* (grouper).

Near here your walk merges with the main Avenida Litoral running through Playa de las Américas. This is the heart of the resort, quietly ticking over by day but racing at night. Between its buildings runs a deep *barranco* marking the boundary between the two *Ayuntiamentos* that compère this show, **Adeje** and **Arona.** Across the border the density of neon signs thickens as you near the **Veronicas** complex, a nerve-centre of around 100 bars that offer their customers all the drink and dance music they can take. There are more bars and clubs across the road, connected by an underpass, including a beacon for young English males, **Gary Lineker's Bar.**

In this part of town the clock is set to PARTY. To do things properly you should really abandon this walk and head for the beach – it's important to rest, as you'll be up all night. Here Happy Hours start at 11pm and end at 1am, and few serious party animals will get to bed before 7am. You should then surface again about lunchtime and continue your snooze by the pool. Have an English breakfast at tea-time. By 9pm it will be time to get dressed and by midnight you should be wide awake and raring to go.

If you've not been trapped by a Fun Pub showing Billy Connolly videos, cut back through the complex to the seafront. Make sure you've had a drink or ice-cream before continuing the walk, which leads away from the packed beaches towards the Las Palmeras Hotel. Along the shore you can see Playa de las Américas' only historical sight, two World War II pill-boxes. Around this promontory the beach is wild and windy with Atlantic rollers sweeping into the coast. It's not safe for swimming but this doesn't deter the surfers – inevitably there are plans to develop here, which accounts for the sporadic graffiti against the *diques* (dykes).

Further on you will reach the striking circular building of Parque Santiago IV – Tenerife's apartment complexes tend to be numbered like the sequels of movie blockbusters. Turn left then right, skirting round this holiday housing estate, and return to the shore. Here you pass beside the bold blue **Mediterranean Palace Hotel,** a five-star luxury establishment that is one of the best on the island. Close by lies the Las Vegas-style Pyrámide de Arona conference centre and casino, part of the Mare Nostrum Resort. Ahead of you is Los Cristianos, gradually being joined to Playa de las Américas as new beaches and palm-lined promenades are built. To its left the cone of Montaña Chayofita is disappearing under a pile of egg-box apartments, while beyond the port more tourist complexes are devouring the immense Montaña Guaza (1,410ft, 430m).

On the outskirts and along the seafront of **Los Cristianos** you will come across several private houses that have defied the on-

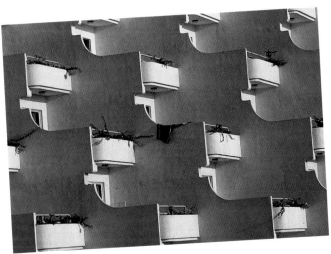

slaught of development, secluded villas and fishermen's cottages that have resolutely shunned the advances of the resort's tower blocks. If you mentally subtract all the modern development around them it's not hard to imagine what the tiny Puerto de Los Cristianos was like for most of this century – a cluster of low, white *casas* huddled round a small mole, occasionally visited by fishing boats and the local steamers and fruit-boats that called to collect the tomatoes grown up on the terraced hills around Arona.

Continue along the seaside walk into Los Cristianos, going through a tunnel and past the Bar Rincón del Marinero. This takes you into the harbour, a peaceful haven for yachts, trawlers and pleasure boats. The four times a day sailing of the *MV Benchijigua* to La Gomera spurs it to life – suddenly taxis scream round the quayside to meet its departure and a procession of greens, hippies and backpackers embark for the alternative paradise of the island's beaches and valleys (see *Option 15*).

Los Cristianos is one of the best places to join one of the many boat and fishing trips available off the south coast (see Option 6 below), and a walk along the quayside is an ideal way to assess what's on offer. The port is at its busiest in the winter months – in November transatlantic sailors flock here to await the trade winds that will carry them across to the Caribbean. The harbour carpark is also a traditional rendezvous for the many caravanners who regularly spend a nomadic winter in the Canary Islands.

As you leave the harbour you will notice a square, cream building known as the **Casa del Mar,** where there is an upstairs restaurant (Tel: 79 32 75, closed Mondays) that offers good international and Canarian food as well as views over the port. Carry on round to Los Cristianos beach where there are numerous bars and pavement cafés suitable for a well-deserved drink. Now it's your turn to sit and watch others walk by. This relaxed and cosmopolitan resort is now considerably more sophisticated than the days when the first package holidaymakers arrived in the mid-1960s – then Los Cristianos was a winding, four-hour drive from Los Rodeos Airport, with only a few hotels, one cinema and an empty beach. You had to wait three days for a foreign newspaper to arrive, there was no television and the only radio signals not blocked by Teide were French broadcasts from Senegal. These days disco music seeps from every bar and the kiosks sell daily newspapers flown in from abroad the same afternoon.

To get back to Playa de las Américas, walk into the centre of town – you will find the taxi rank and bus station up on the Carretera Los Cristianos.

With few natural attractions and no historical sights, Tenerife's southern resorts have to work hard to entertain their guests. The

sea is the south's major asset and **boat trips** offer some of the best excursions available. They fall into two types, those that are into fun and those that are after fish. Pleasure cruises, pirate voyages, sangria sailings and so on are normally part- or all-day jollies with food included, a time for drinking in the sun and dancing on the waves. These operate from the harbours at **Los Cristianos, Puerto Colón, San Juan** and **Los Gigantes.** Dolphin and whale chases, deep-sea fishing, shark-hunting expeditions etc are more expensive, more exciting and usually for an all-day, all-in price. Los Gigantes, Los Cristianos and Puerto Colón are the main harbours for this.

Paradoxically, the aquatic attraction that always draws the crowds is the wholly artificial **Octopus Aguapark** in **San Eugenio Alto** (Playa de las Américas). Open all year (daily 10am–6pm, free bus, adult admission 1,200ptas, children and OAPs 700ptas), it's an open-air adventure swimming pool with an exciting range of slides and rides – save it up though, for if you take the kids on your first day they won't want to go anywhere else!

Safaris are another popular way to make the desert look lively. You can watch it undulate from the back of a camel (**Camel Safari Guaza,** east of Los Cristianos) or tear across it in a jeep (many companies). If you prefer to see it spin, try **Karting Las Americas,** a popular go-kart track on the northern outskirts of town (open daily 9am–7pm, free bus). You could also try an aerial view (**Skyride Parascending,** based at Playa Troya, Playa de las Américas), and don't forget the underwater perspective (**Yellow Submarine,** Las Galletas), from a 43-seater Finnish submarine that makes regular dives off Tenerife's southwestern tip (daily from 10am, free bus). Near Los Cristanos, La Aguilas del Teide is an impressive new eco-park with wild animals, birds of prey and live shows.

La Laguna

After defeating the Guanches in 1496, De Lugo established his capital on the high inland plateau between Teide and the Anaga mountains. Known as **San Cristóbal de la Laguna,** the original site was beside a lake *(laguna)* that has since disappeared. Today it is a modern city whose outskirts are gradually merging with those of Santa Cruz, the port that took over as the island's capital in 1723. Its growth has been phenomenal: in 1930 there were 20,000 inhabitants, today there are 120,000.

For all this development La Laguna remains firmly De Lugo's town. Its ancient inner core still bears the hallmark of the Renaissance grid of narrow streets he laid down five centuries ago, early town planning that was to be repeated throughout Spanish America. In fact, some Andalucian emigrants destined for the New World travelled no further than La Laguna, seduced by its refreshing altitude and the fertile soil of the surrounding valleys.

La Laguna

Today, La Laguna is a city to wander in and enjoy. It has no overwhelming sights—its merits are more subtle and atmospheric. Like many of the provincial towns back on the *meseta* that were enriched by *conquistador* gold, it displays its history casually: a stone coat-of-arms emblazons a mansion wall, a heavy wooden door opens to reveal a timeless inner *patio* and gurgling fountain, a Canary balcony sags with the weight of years, still blushing with geraniums.

It also has a placid, cultural air, a legacy of its learned and enlightened past. A university was established here as early as 1701 and today its students add a youthful vitality to the ancient streets. Their exuberance is kept in check by the large numbers of clerics you'll see conferring beneath lampposts and sidestepping the traffic—La Laguna has been the seat of an episcopal see since 1818 and the city continues to play host to many religious orders.

Like Santa Cruz, La Laguna makes few concessions for tourists. If you want to see inside its churches and buildings you will have to come during the morning or early evening, though it's equally pleasurable to stroll through its empty streets during the siesta. Parking is a headache here – try to find a space within sight of the towers of the cathedral or Nuestra Señora de la Concepción and walk in.

La Laguna's centrepiece is its cathedral, **Santa Iglesia.** Although it was founded in 1515, the present neoclassical building only dates from 1904, crowned by a dome and twin towers whose structure is now challenged by some precariously tall palm trees. Some years ago its white exterior was painted pink, a source of much local controversy. The interior is confidently ornate as the sunlight slips through stained-glass windows to illuminate the nave and its slender pillars draped with red damask hangings. The cathedral's marble pulpit dates from 1767. To the right of the altar lies the tomb of the city's father, Alonso Fernández de Lugo, *'Conquistador de Tenerife y Palma'.*

From the front of the cathedral head left up Calle Obispo Rey Redondo to the **Plaza de la Concepción,** where you will pass what must be one of the most opulent electricity sub-stations in the world. Ahead of you rises the six-tier tower of the **Iglesia de Nuestra Señora de la Concepción,** a national monument. Built in 1502, it was one of the island's first churches, though the present tower dates from 1701. The main entrance is on the opposite side in Plaza Dr Oliviera. Open only for Masses and from 5-6.30pm, its long, narrow nave supports a decorously carved and painted wooden ceiling that exemplifies the Tinerfeños' long tradition of fine woodwork. Look for an alcove to the side that contains a 15th-century green glazed font used to baptise the Guanche chieftains. Above it are family trees tracing the lineages that have descended from those it has blessed.

Return to the foot of the church tower and take Calle Belén through to Plaza Junta Suprema. Here you turn right on the long **Calle San Agustín.** This street contains many of La Laguna's stately homes and religious buildings, some of which are now used for cultural and administrative purposes.

On your left you will pass the **Instituto de Cabrera Pinto** (with the bell tower) where craft fairs are often held, followed by the historic San Agustín monastery. Beyond the junction with Calle Sol y Ortega is the Palacio Episcopal (No. 28), and opposite (No. 23), the **Universidad de San Fernando,** the site

Santa Iglesia

La Laguna, 1900

of La Laguna's first university, founded by Augustinian canons.

Just past the university, a left turn down Calle Tabares de Cala takes you to one of La Laguna's largest squares, **Plaza San Francisco.** Here you will find the **Santuario del Cristo,** part of a Franciscan friary standing next door to a military barracks. Their two well-kept entrances, guarded diligently by soldiers or beggars, seem to be offering visitors a choice between war and peace. Inside the Santuario is a narrow chapel, a cool place of solace and pilgrimage that houses a long-venerated figure of Christ, *Santísimo Cristo de la Laguna.* The statue, made by a Sevillan sculptor in the 15th century and brought to Tenerife by De Lugo in 1520, now stands wreathed in gold and silver, a powerful image to this day.

From the bottom of the Plaza walk back down Calle Nava y Grimón. This takes you to the historic **Plaza del Adelantado,** where several bars offer the chance for a drink. Alternatively, if you pop into the **Mercado** (open 8am–1pm) you can buy a cake or some

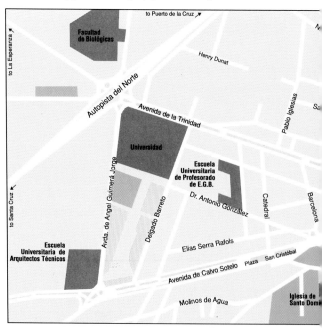

fruit and sit outside on a laurel-shaded bench as you contemplate the Plaza's buildings. With their Canary balconies and Spanish Colonial coats-of-arms they present a composite guide to the island's architecture.

The Plaza's name, Adelantado (literally 'the advanced one'), refers to the title bestowed on De Lugo after the conquest. At one corner stands the 19th-century *Ayuntiamento* with its regulation neoclassical façade; inside is the flag planted by De Lugo when he claimed Tenerife for Spain.

On the opposite corner from the Town Hall, next to the Santa Catalina convent, is the squat **Palacio de Nava,** a baroque mansion that was once the hub of La Laguna's cultural life. In the early 18th century it was the home of the Marquis of Villanueva del Prado, whose salon was attended by all the island's leading thinkers – his son founded the Botanical Gardens in Puerto de la Cruz.

Diagonally opposite the Palacio de Nava is the house where Father José de Anchieta was born in 1534 (marked by a plaque). He was a Jesuit missionary who went to Brazil and is said to have converted two million Indians to Christianity. A monument to this dubious achievement stands beside the Autopista del Norte (close

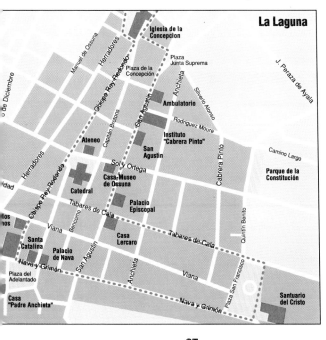

to the junction where you turn off to enter La Laguna), where drivers are assailed by a stiff-backed statue of this Apostle of Brazil.

Next door to Father Anchieta's house is the **Hotel Nivaria** (No. 11) which has a cool, modern and history-free bar. It does serve snacks, but for a good meal you'll have to head up to the restaurants around La Esperanza or along the old C820 towards Puerto de la Cruz (see *Dining Experiences*).

8. La Orotava Town Walk (two hours)

La Orotava has always had a genteel air, in keeping with its elevated position (1,100ft, 335m) overlooking the fertile Valle de la Orotava. Originally known as Araotava, it was once a major Guanche settlement in the richest of their kingdoms, Taora. After the conquest, its strategic location and equable climate appealed to the Spanish settlers and by the early 16th century it was a burgeoning colonial town. A small port was constructed below to export the valley's produce, Puerto de la Orotava, which four centuries later ballooned into the high-rise resort of Puerto de la Cruz.

La Orotava's social graces are preserved in the clutch of cobbled streets and 18th-century mansions around its old town centre. You need only linger a couple of hours in this *'villa muy noble y leal'*, 'most loyal and noble town' as it modestly declares on its coat-of-arms, but in that time you'll see Tenerife at its most charming.

Mid-morning is a good time to visit. If you're driving up from Puerto de la Cruz (C821) follow the road as it climbs through the modern town, turning right by a Shell garage (and a tall pine)

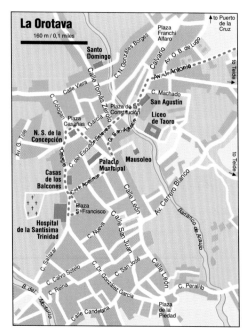

where you should then park as soon as possible. This road is **Avenida José Antonio,** a wide street that leads off from the main Puerto de la Cruz–Las Cañadas road (C821).

Head towards the old town centre via this street, which becomes the Carrera del Escultor Estévez as you pass a large ochre building, the San Augustín monastery (1648). Soon you are in the **Plaza de la Constitución,** the town's social centre, bordered by a parapet offering views of the valley below. You'll find a pleasant example of the Canarios' capacity to turn everything into a bar under the bandstand, an ideal spot for coffee.

Iglesia de Nuestra Señora de la Concepción

Continue along the Carrera del Escultor Estévez into **Plaza de General Franco,** dominated by the neoclassical façade of the Palacio Municipal (1871). Every year the broad square in front is painstakingly decorated with extravagant floral carpets celebrating Corpus Christi (see *Special Events*). Made from local flowers and the volcanic sands of Las Cañadas, their vivid depiction of religious scenes have been a feature of La Orotava's devotions since the 1840s.

On the corner of the Plaza, Calle Tomás Pérez leads to the town's principal church, **Iglesia de Nuestra Señora de la Concepción.** Founded in 1503, the first church on this site was destroyed by an earthquake in 1705 and the present baroque edifice dates from 1768. Its interior is cool and restful, lit only by the sunlight streaming through the stained-glass of its windows and dome.

Walk round to the rear of the church and up the steep Calle Colegio into **Calle San Francisco.** These cobbled streets will lead you past some fine Canary mansions, including the beautiful **Casa de los Balcones** (No. 3). Built in 1632, its carved wood balconies and inner *patio* are some of the best preserved in the island. For the last 50 years it has been an embroidery school and it still has some 20 students learning the art. Once every village and town in the Canaries had its own pattern used for its open threadwork *(calados),* and today Casa de los Balcones works hard to save these designs for the future. The school produces some of the most impressive embroidery *(bordados)* in the Canary Islands and this is one of the best places to buy it. Tablecloths with napkins are a popular buy, but you can also pick up exquisite handkerchiefs for the bargain price of a few hundred pesetas.

Further up Calle San Francisco you will find the large **Hospital de la Santísima Trinidad** next to the triangular Plaza San Francisco.

Built in 1600 as a Franciscan convent, it has been a hospital since 1884 and its peaceful cloisters are open to visitors (10.30am–12noon and 4–5.30pm). The balcony by its entrance has splendid views over the Orotava valley, and within the hospital's tall front doors you'll see a revolving wooden drum where foundling babies and children could be abandoned anonymously.

At the bottom of Plaza San Francisco turn right down Calle Hermano Apolinar. This takes you alongside the delightful and rarely visited **Hijuela de Botánico** (open 8am–2pm, closed Sundays and holidays). The entrance is round the corner in Calle Tomas Pérez. Laid down in 1923, the Hijuela (daughter) is a small off-shoot of the Jardín de Aclimatación in Puerto de la Cruz (see Option 4), a mini-paradise of exotic plants that includes a dragon tree and a number of now rare and endangered Canary palms.

From the entrance to the gardens walk across the street to turn left down Calle León, then right into the winding Calle San Agustín. This takes you past the grounds of an aristocratic mansion, the Liceo de Taoro (a private club), and into Plaza de la Constitución. From here you can walk back to Avenida José Antonio.

9. Icod and San Marcos

This is an itinerary for a classic Tenerife day, visiting one of the island's most famous sights then retiring to the beach for a fish lunch and swim. It's very easy-going and if you prefer to do more you could call in at Icod *en route* to Teno (see *Day 2 Itinerary: Macizo de Teno*) or combine it with a visit to Garachico nearby (see *Option 10, page 72*).

Icod de los Vinos is on the island's north coast at the junction of the C820 and TF142. It's one of Tenerife's oldest towns, founded by the Spanish in 1501 but originally a Guanche settlement aptly known as Benicod, meaning 'beautiful place'. It has long been a

Icod's Dragon Tree

centre for viticulture and you can still buy bottles of its *vinos* – the white, such as the 'La Guancha' or 'Icod' labels, are generally agreed to be the most palatable.

Icod's star attraction is its ancient **Drago Milenario**, a giant dizzy-branched dragon tree reputed to be between 2,000 and 3,000 years old (directions to it are signposted). Regularly blitzed by coach parties and almost felled by traffic, it nevertheless remains an impressive sight, defiantly mushrooming over everyone's heads like an atom bomb cloud. The best views of it are from the balustrades of the shady Plaza de Andrés de L. Cáceres nearby. There is some speculation as to El Drago's real age (it may only be 500 years old) but with a trunk now some 56ft (17m) high and 20ft (6m) round, its grandeur is without question.

The Guanches held their dragon trees in high reverence, regarding them as a symbol of fertility and sagacity and making shields from their bark. The resin — which turns red when exposed to the air — was known to the medieval world as dragon's blood and valued for its medicinal properties. Later it was used as a dye to varnish musical instruments, stain marble and as a cosmetic.

Walk up the narrow cobbled Calle Arcipreste Ossuna towards the old town, a gaggle of white houses graced by Canary balconies and terracotta roofs. The **Plaza de la Constitución** is one of the loveliest squares in Tenerife with a fountain surrounded by palms, laurels and oleander. If you continue up the hill along Calle San Antonio you'll get a clear sight up to Teide and the chance to see a second dragon tree in the **Plaza José Manuel Cabrera**. This is a quiet spot to pause and take in the view of the *barranco* below, lush with bananas and palms.

Black beach, San Marcos

Returning to the Plaza de la Constitución, you'll see several souvenir and crafts shops selling straw and wooden baskets and terracotta pottery. **Artesania Tajinaste** is the best, a good opportunity to buy some presents — perhaps a hand-made shawl or some pottery or lace. The shop also stocks natural perfumes made from Tenerife's flowers, including rose, *strelitzia* and *retama del Teide*.

Drop back down to the Plaza de Andrés de L. Cáceres, shadowed by a magnificent variety of ancient trees, including a gargantuan *ficus macrophylla*. The 16th-century Iglesia de San Marcos stands nearby. Back beside El Drago, the **Casa de Drago** sells every conceivable Tenerife souvenir, including giant Canary cigars and banana harmonicas. Across the road the terrace bar of the **Hostal del Drago** is an ideal spot to view El Drago with the cone of Teide behind. The bar also sells seeds and baby versions of *dracaena draco* if you fancy a long-term investment.

From the Drago Milenario take the road downhill, turning left by the Shell garage then right to follow the signs to **Playa de San Marcos**. Once a tiny fishing port, San Marcos is now developing into a resort — it's best to park before you reach the harbour and walk down. There is a small black beach and two promenades of bars and fish restaurants. This is a place to relax and enjoy the sun and sea breezes — if you arrive early you can sometimes see fishing boats being hoisted out of the water and the day's catch sold.

San Marcos is a good place to try a *paella* (2,000ptas for two). Its restaurants are modern and characteristically unpretentious, the fish excellent — try some *mero, cherne* or *sargo* (see Eating Out). **Bar-Restaurante Maritimo** (Tel: 82 27 02) is recommended.

Castillo de San Miguel

Garachico is a small, historic gem set into Tenerife's north-western shore, well worth a visit if you're *en route* to Teno or Icod. A gentle town with a dramatic past, its narrow streets are packed with 18th century houses and religious buildings ideal for an afternoon or early evening stroll. If the sun's out you could easily stay longer, enjoying a fish lunch or a swim in its protected pools.

Up until 1706 Garachico was Tenerife's main port, a natural anchorage where wealthy Genoese merchants settled as the island's sugar and wine trade flourished. Then on 5 May an eruption of El Volcán Negro sent a sea of molten lava rolling towards the coast. Fortunately, its gradual advance was slow enough to allow the town's inhabitants time to evacuate and there was no loss of life.

However, the port was completely swamped and only a few buildings survived. For a good view of the lava's fan of devastation go up to the Mirador de Garachico above – take the C820 towards El Tanque (see Day 2 Itinerary: Macizo de Teno).

Garachico was subsequently rebuilt, its elegant cobbled streets following the curve of lava that now spreads into the sea. Today the town is a quiet and cultured haven that has managed to resist the ugly lava of tourist development now flowing round the coast.

10. Garachico Town Walk (one hour)

Park along the seafront. The walk begins by the charming **Castillo de San Miguel,** a 16th-century fortification with thick stone walls that successfully withstood the onslaught of Teide's lava. It's now a craft shop selling embroidery and metalwork (open 10am–7pm daily). If you go up onto the roof you'll be able to trace the route of the lava as it flowed down the cliffs and into the sea.

Opposite the Castillo is the well-known **Isla Baja** restaurant where you can stop for a drink or buy an *helado* to help you tour the town. If you smoke, pop round the corner into Calle José Antonio where a small shop, **Artesanales Arturo,** still makes hand-rolled cigars from locally-grown tobacco.

Next to the Isla Baja an alley leads through into the crescent-shaped cobbled street, **Estaban de Ponte.** This is worth exploring a little (turn left) to get a feel of the town's modest 18th century houses, neatly painted white and brown. You'll then need to retrace your steps and turn left up Calle José Calvo Sotelo into the Plaza Glorieta de San Francisco. One corner of this has been commandeered by the **Convento de San Francisco,** another building that survived the eruption. Today it is a **Casa de Cultura** (Cultural Centre) and regularly holds exhibitions and events. Open 8am–1pm and 2–7pm, it's worth looking inside to see its well-restored cloisters and a small natural history museum with exhibits that include an interesting aerial photograph of the lava flows around Garachico.

Further round the Plaza you'll see the dark, heavy stone of the mid-17th century **Casa Palacio de los Condes de la Gomera.** The former residence of the Marquises of La Gomera and Adeje, most of it survived the lava-flows and is now due for restoration. Nearby is the 18th-century Iglesia de Santa Ana

18th-century church

and a modern square containing a statue to the South American liberator Simón Bolívar, whose mother came from Garachico.

Carry on past the Iglesia down into the Plaza de Juan González de la Torre. On one side are some sunken gardens containing the **Puerta de Tierra,** a stone gateway to the town erected in 1600 that has since been dug out from the lava. Near to it is a truly enormous *lagar* (wine press) dating from the 17th century, testimony to the days when the Malvasia wine trade dominated the island.

From the Plaza you can walk back past Artesanales Arturo to the seafront.

11. Adeje and the Barranco del Infierno

Set high in the hills overlooking Playa de las Américas, **Adeje** keeps a wise distance from the holiday playgrounds it now governs. Once a Guanche capital from which the whole island was ruled, this quiet town still conducts its affairs with distinction. Adeje is also the gateway to the Barranco del Infierno (Hell's Gorge), the deepest ravine in the Canaries. You can walk to its heart and back in two and a half hours, but avoid going in the midday heat and take stout footwear.

Adeje lies 7 miles (11.3km) north of Playa de las Américas – take the main C822 then turn off to climb up to the town (TF 5116). A fine avenue of laurels runs through its centre to a 16th century church, Santa Ursula. The road then bears left past the **Casa Fuerte,** once a fortified mansion occupied by the Counts of La Gomera, who owned a vast sugar plantation worked by over 1,000 Negro slaves. Built in 1556, it was sacked 30 years later by English pirates and was then all but destroyed by fire in the 19th century. Today a 16th-century cannon stands outside the building, too heavy to be melted down during the Spanish Civil War.

The road continues uphill to the entrance to the **Barranco del**

Infierno. A winding path leads you into the ravine, cut to a deep 'v' by erosion. Its start is not promising, for you find yourself entering a baking hot, rocky gorge punctuated with prickly pear and the gaping holes of Guanche caves. Gradually you find yourself dropping down into a cool, leafy tunnel thick with bramble and willow and welcomingly watered by a stream. The path culminates in the sheer walls of the gorge where in winter a waterfall cascades down to a small pool.

On your return you can quench your thirst at the **Bar-Restaurante Otelo,** which also serves good Canarian food.

12. El Médano and Los Abrigos

Some of Tenerife's best natural beaches can be found near **El Médano,** 12 miles (19.3km) east of Playa de las Américas. Not far from here the tiny quay at **Los Abrigos** is the focus for a shoal of fish restaurants that serve Canarian seafood at its simplest and most perfect. If you feel like an easy-going day, try a long walk along these breezy shores followed by an even longer fish lunch. If you like more action El Médano is also a windsurfer's paradise, regularly used for international competitions, while nearby are two of the island's PGA-approved golf courses (see *Sport* section).

To get to El Médano from Playa de las Américas, take the *autopista* east towards Santa Cruz, turning off at the next exit after the airport. A straight road leads down to the town but turn right just as you're about to enter, following signs to Los Abrigos (TF6214). Pull off and park near the Hotel Playa Sur Tenerife. **Playa de Médano** lies ahead of you. This part of the bay catches the full force of the north-east trade winds – *los alisios* – and its surf is often a dazzling kaleidoscope of windsurfers' sails. It's not for the inexperienced though, and the safest place to swim is to your left, on the safe beach in front of El Médano town.

To your right lies the neat red cinder cone of **Montaña Roja,** which you can walk up unless the winds are very strong. Beyond this lie two more beaches, **La Tejita** and **El Confital,** that get increasingly deserted as you proceed west, either by driving along a track or walking. Out here the desert is wild and Saharan and, not surprisingly, a hot-bed for UFO sightings.

Continue along the road to Los Abrigos. Soon you reach a right turning marked **Hermano Pedro.** This small detour takes you to the eastern end of the airport runway beneath which is a remarkable cave devoted to a 17th-century hermit and founder of the Bethlehemite religious order. Born in 1619 in Vilaflor, Hermano Pedro (Brother Peter) appears to have led an ascetic, cave-dwelling existence before emigrating to Guatemala where he attracted many religious followers. Canonised in 1980, he is now that nation's patron saint and this obscure cave is the object of an annual pilgrimage. In the past its walls were papered with photographs of the loved and lost. Worshippers would leave crutches and even green Spanish L-plates as a thanks offering for Hermano Pedro's assistance in passing a driving test. Today only a respectful array of candles and flowers can be seen.

Return to the road and turn right, continuing until you reach the breezeblock town now growing around **Los Abrigos**. Park near its central junction and walk down to the sea. Here you will find a small harbour lined with fish restaurants. All are good and offer much the same food, so just pick one with the sun or shade to suit you. This is the place to eat fish and seafood – the waiter will lead you to a fridge where you simply pick out your choice, which is sold by weight (see *Dining Experiences*). Ask for *papas arrugadas* and *mojo* sauce. A meal for two costs from 4,500ptas, but you'll probably want to splash out on some good Spanish wine and a life-enhancing Mallorcan dessert. By the way, if you see other people eating and drinking like the world is ending tomorrow, it's because they're having a last beano before reeling towards the airport and a soporific flight home.

13. Candelaria

In 1392 two Guanche shepherds are said to have discovered a Holy Image of the Virgin among the rocks of Playa del Socorro, holding a naked child and a candle. The shepherds sent word of this to their king, the Mencey of Güimar, who had the statue taken to a cave at Chinguaro where it became an object of veneration known as *'Chaxiraxi'*.

Candelaria basilica

Almost six hundred years later the Image of Nuestra Señora de la Candelaria sits high above the altar of a capacious basilica, the object of an annual pilgrimage (August 14–15) that brings thousands of devotees from all over the Canaries to fill the vast square outside. That same day candles are lit in the hundreds of churches that now bear her name throughout South America, for from such miraculous origins a

75

The Virgin of Candelaria

worldwide cult has grown.

About 12 miles (19.3km) south of Santa Cruz (well signposted on the Autopista del Sur), **Candelaria** is Tenerife's principal religious site. The town's small fishing harbour and the semi-developed resort beside it give little indication of the imposing basilica you will find at its western end, completed in 1959 (closed 1–3pm). The large square in front of the basilica is overseen by ten rough-hewn statues of Guanche kings, regularly baptised by the sea in stormy weather.

Discovered a century before the Spanish invasion, the Image of Our Lady was to play a key role in the conversion of the island to the Catholic church. Dominican monks who arrived in 1530 took over the shrine, which was by then in the Cave de San Blas (further along the seafront). Caring for the statue proved a difficult task: in 1789 the Virgin had to be rescued from a fire in a nearby church and then in 1826, after the church had been rebuilt, a tidal wave broke in and swept her out to sea. What you see today is therefore a copy of Our Lady, made shortly after her disappearance. In 1867 she was made patron saint of all the Canary Islands and the long marble aisle of the basilica is rarely empty of suppliant worshippers shuffling towards the altar on their knees.

For some bodily nourishment to complement your spiritual edification, wander to the end of Candelaria's main street, Calle Obispo Pérez Cáceres, where an ice-cream from **Carlo's** (No. 49) or a cake from **Torre le Paz** (No. 50) will work more wonders. Up the hill overlooking the basilica you'll find the old part of Candelaria, quiet streets of low white houses that have hardly changed in a century.

14. Beaches

For an island with such a reputation for 'sun and sea' holidays, it's surprising to learn how few natural beaches there are on Tenerife. Black sand, pebbly shorelines and strong currents are rarely mentioned in the holiday brochures and many visitors are disappointed to discover that there are few golden swathes of sand comparable to those at Mediterranean or British resorts.

To counteract this shortcoming, the Tinerfeños have worked hard, importing vast quantities of Saharan sand to create artificial beaches and building ingenious seawater pools that allow swimmers to enjoy the ocean's swell in safety. If you like to venture beyond the hotel pool, this is a brief guide to some of the best places to swim on Tenerife, including beaches and artificial pools.

Playa de las Teresitas: Just north of Santa Cruz by San Andrès, this is the island's most classic beach, a long bow of clean golden sand created in 1970 simply by bringing three and a half million cubic feet (98,000m³) of it over from the Spanish Sahara. A city beach, it has full amenities but it can get rather busy at weekends.

Las Gaviotas: Continue north from Las Teresitas towards Igueste (TF1121), and the beach is in the next bay over the mountain. Set at the base of steep cliffs, Las Gaviotas ('the Seagulls') is a narrow strip of black sand met by foaming waves. This beach is especially popular with the young and nudism is tolerated.

Puerto de la Cruz: To the west of Castillo de San Felipe, Playa Jardín is a wide, family beach with grey sand.

Playa de la Arena: Clean, black sand beach in self-contained resort to the south of Puerto de Santiago.

Playa de Médano: Three miles (5km) of fair sand on the southwest coast, popular with windsurfers – see *Option 12, page 74.*

Playa de las Américas/Los Cristianos: A chain of busy, man-improved beaches linking the two resorts. In Playa de las Américas there are two beaches to the west of the marina (Torviscas, Marina) and another two (Playa del Bobo, Playas de Troya) near the Veronicas complex. Further east a new beach has recently been created beside the Mediterranean Place Hotel, and another at Nuevo Mar, where you can windsurf. On the west side of Los Cristianos, Playa de Teno is a wide arc of imported sand which is sheltered by breakwaters.

There are also fine black sand beaches at **San Marcos** (below Icod, see *Option 9, page 71*) and **Poris de Abona** (turn off halfway down the Autopista del Sur).

For artificial seaside pools, the **Lago de Martiánez** in Puerto de la Cruz is outstanding (see *Option 4, page 54*) and there are also good seawater pools at **Bajamar** and **Garachico,** both on the north coast of the island.

15. Day Trip to La Gomera

La Gomera is only 20 miles (32km) southwest of Tenerife, but it's another world. It remains relatively unspoiled (though its days are surely numbered) and if you make the short sea voyage there you'll be able to enjoy a genuine, pre-MacDonalds Canary Island. Known as the 'Isla de Cordialidad', this friendly island is small, circular and mountainous, scarred by deep ravines that slice down to a rocky shoreline. A lush vegetation tempers the violence of the landscape, cloaking the mountain peaks with cool forests of laurel and

Ferry to Gomera

cedar and lining the valley floors with plantations thick with guavas, mangoes, avocados and bananas.

The islanders, known as Gomeros, are a gentle people who retain the tranquil traditions of Canarian life. Some still practise a unique whistling language, called *silbo,* used to communicate across the steep terrain.

An airport is currently being built on La Gomera, the last Canary Island to get one. If you're staying in Playa de las Américas or Los Cristianos it's easily visited in a day trip, but if you're coming from Puerto de la Cruz consider staying overnight in the idyllic four-star **Parador Nacional de la Gomera** in San Sebastián (Tel: 87 11 00).

Hotels and travel agents organise coach excursions to La Gomera but you can quite easily go independently. The most leisurely way across to the island is by the ferry *M.V. Benchijigua,* operated by Ferry Gomera (Tel: 79 05 56). You can take your car, but you will find it more relaxing to go on foot and then tour the island by taxi. Be sure to get the first sailing from the quayside at Los Cristianos, which leaves at 9am sharp (the next crossings are at 12.30pm, 4pm and 8pm, no midday sailings on Wednesday). The 80-minute sea voyage is invigorating and you may see dolphins and flying fish along the way.

The small harbour of San Sebastián, La Gomera's capital, was Columbus' last port of call before setting off to discover Cuba in 1492. Its narrow streets and shady squares still have a feel of those pioneer days and the town's principal fortification, a 15th century tower called the Torre del Conde, was originally used to house

Gomera landscape

booty brought back from the New World by the *conquistadores*.

San Sebastián's main square, **Plaza de la Constitución**, is the place to negotiate your island tour with a taxi driver. There are also buses to various parts of the island that meet the ferry but you'll have to take them as soon as you disembark. Gomeran taxi drivers are a friendly, honest bunch – a full island tour will cost around 7,500ptas and you should offer to buy lunch for your driver/guide.

Be sure to visit the primeval forests of the **Parque Nacional de Garajonay,** which contain some of the world's oldest trees recognised by UNESCO. There is a Visitor Centre at Juego de Bolas with gardens and demonstrations of local handicrafts. You should also make the hair-raising descent to **Valle Gran Rey,** a steep, intensively cultivated valley that culminates in some small black sand beaches and is overlooked by the Mirador del Palmarejo.

Allow plenty of time for your return journey to San Sebastián, as the last ferry back to Los Cristianos leaves at 6pm (other sailings at 7am, 10.45am and 2.15pm (there is no afternoon sailing on Wednesday).

Gomera terracing

Eating out in Tenerife has improved greatly since the Guanches first knelt down to Sunday lunch. They survived on goat and *gofio,* their pots occasionally enlivened by partridge, quail or wildcat. Many islanders continue to use *gofio* – a finely ground, toasted wheat or maize flour – and some restaurants serve it with soups or main dishes.

Today the island caters to all tastes. In the tourist resorts – where the British and Germans tend to rule – egg and bacon breakfasts and bratwurst and sauerkraut suppers are the norm. Here you can always eat well, if unexceptionally. Meals are invariably good value, with generous portions served virtually all day and often

well into the night. Menus come signposted with national flags and the dessert trolley is a photograph album. Be sure to entertain yourself with the amusing translations *(lapas a la plancha* – limpets – sometimes appears as 'grilled slime') and don't ask for the *menú del día* (menu of the day) when you really mean the *especialidad del día* (speciality of the day) – the first is a low price set-meal all restaurants must offer by law, the latter is whatever is fresh and in season.

For a truly Canarian meal head straight to the fish restaurants. Ideally, you should drive out to one of the small ports that are nothing but fish restaurants, such as **Los Abrìgos** (see Option 12)

and **San Juan** in the south or **San Marcos** (see Option 9) and **Playa del Roque** (see Itinerary 3) in the north. Go for lunch – the main meal of the day, taken around 2pm – but be sure to schedule yourself a siesta afterwards. You'll also find excellent fish restaurants in the main resorts, good for a quiet evening meal after a hard day's sightseeing. Dinner is normally served from 8pm but at weekends many Canario-run establishments don't get going until later.

Such restaurants often have no menu, just a procession of customers wandering into the kitchen to inspect the day's catch. Waiters are proud to explain the merits of each fish, which after selection will be weighed and cooked to your directions. Grilled is often best *(a la plancha)* and don't be afraid to ask for a large fish to be divided between two people – in Spain you can dine unshackled by etiquette, eating however much you want in whatever order pleases your palate.

Look out for these local fish: *mero, abade, cabrilla* and *cherne* are all members of the sea bass family. *Mero* and *abade* are very common, white, flakey fish known to us as groupers; *cherne* is larger, a delicious and firm wreckfish often served as a steak. *Salmón* is red mullet. *Sama* is a large, deep-bodied fish and *sargo* and *chopa* are similar, both fleshy seabream. *Vieja* is a local name for parrotfish. Then there are the better known fish – *sardinas, atún* and *bonito* (skipjack tuna), and probably the best of the lot, *lenguado,* sole. Other familiar seafood includes prawns *(gambas),* squid *(calamares),* octopus *(pulpo),* shrimps *(camarones),* mussels *(mejillones),* limpets *(lapas)* and giant deep-sea prawns *(langostinos).*

To accompany this, order *ensalada* (salad) and *papas arrugadas,* small Canary potatoes cooked in their jackets in well-salted water and served with a piquant *mojo* sauce. *Mojo* comes either *rojo* (red), spiced with red peppers, garlic, cummin and saffron, or *verde* (green), which is milder and based on parsley and coriander.

Canary cuisine is far more than fish though. Inland, the restaurants serve succulent meat dishes: slabs of steak *(solomillo)* that overhang the plate in true South American style, lamb cooked in oil and garlic *(cordero al ajillo),* roast kid *(cabrito asado),* rabbit served in a spicy sauce *(conejo en salmorejo)* and charcoal-grilled chicken *(pollo a la brassa).* The best places to eat these are in the north of the island, grouped around **La Esperanza** and **Agua García** and along the old C820 running directly parallel to the Autopista del Norte (TF5), between **Tacoronte** and **La Laguna.** This road contains some of the island's top meat restaurants, packed out at weekends with joyous family banquets that never seem to end – **La Vara** (Tel: 56 38 20) and **Los Limoneros** (Tel: 63 66 27) both at Los Naranjeros, are good examples.

The most authentic Canarian restaurants describe themselves as *típico* and if you want to eat local always go for these. Expect unsophisticated decor and unpretentious food. Look out also for *parrillas* (grills), mostly found in the north and known locally as 'chicken garages', family-run affairs often set up in the garage where meat and poultry are cooked over wood-burning stoves and charcoal grills.

You'll find vegetables don't figure much on Canarian menus but salad is ubiquitous and cheap. If you want variety, experiment with some *tapas* (snacks) or have a starter – perhaps some soup made from fish *(sopa de pescado),* garlic *(de ajos)* or vegetables *(rancho canario).* Desserts are usually a choice of fresh fruit or ice-cream but if you go to a high class Canarian restaurant you can dither over exquisite mousses, *tarta de almendras* (almond tart), *tocino de cielo* (caramel custard) and *nuezes garapiñadas* (walnut brittle).

Prices for a meal range from 1,200ptas a head in a *parrilla* to 2,500ptas in a good fish restaurant and 4,000ptas for a slap-up roast Sunday lunch at a top inland restaurant. Always have some cash in reserve, as not all restaurants take credit cards.

Drinks

Of all the early inhabitants of the Canary Islands, only the Bimbaches on El Hierro were smart enough to produce an alcoholic liquor. They made it from laurel berries and today the island's wine, *vino herreño,* is considered one of the archipelago's best. Wine is still produced in large quantities on Tenerife too, mainly for local consumption. To try some, just ask in a bar for *uno vaso de vino tinto* or *blanco;* if you order *vino de casa* in a small restaurant, it'll most likely come in a soft drink bottle filled straight from the barrel.

Tenerife was once an important source of Canary Sack, the rich Malvasia wine that besotted much of Europe and America between the 16th and 18th centuries. Today the best wines, notably Riojas, are imported from the Spanish mainland, but a few local ones still make their mark – look for the award-winning Viña Norte from El Sauzal. Spanish champagne *(cava)* is also an excellent buy – try the Delapierre or Freixenet labels. Sangria is an over-lauded concoction for tourists and should be treated with caution.

Doradá is the local lager *(cerveza);* if you want draught ask for a *caña. Ron* is the local spirit, a white rum made on Tenerife from sugar cane and often mixed with Coca-cola. You may also meet the sweet *ron miel,* a dark liqueur made from rum and honey, and *cobana,* a banana liqueur that proves a popular souvenir. The Canarians have also made an art out of imitating well-known brands of spirits – Larios gin is the best known, mainly because most of the island's ex-pat community run on it.

Ice is unlikely to be from bottled water and if you want to avoid it ask for your drink *sin hielo. Zumos* are fruit juices freshly-squeezed before your eyes – try a mix of *naranja* (orange) and *limon* (lemon). Bottled water is either *agua con gas* (with bubbles) or *sin gas.* Black coffee is *café solo,* white *con leche.*

Shopping

Tenerife is not a place to set out on a whole day's shopping spree. Afternoon closing tends to cramp the spendthrift's style and while there's no shortage of shops or goods, they can get rather repetitive. If you're only here for a short stay you'd do better to spend the time on the beach and your money in the fish restaurants. Just pick things up as you come across them, or head straight for the best buys described below.

You'll find credit cards and Eurocheques are widely accepted in the tourist resorts, but in smaller villages and isolated shops they only understand cash. There's no need to bargain unless you're in an Asian-run 'tax free' shop or dealing with Tenerife's itinerant salesforce of gypsies, hippies and African hawkers – even then it usually depends on whether both parties can be bothered.

In some supermarkets you have to leave your bag at a counter while you shop. In the smaller shops service can often be excruciatingly slow, though your purchases will come so lovingly wrapped you'll have to forgive them.

Prices and Duty Free

Spain is no longer the cheap shopper's paradise it once was. Prices are similar to those in the UK, with the exception of certain items such as alcohol, tobacco, perfume and watches. Leather goods, ceramic plates and pottery are good value. Some items, such as clothes and household goods imported from the mainland, cost more but keep an eye out for the sales – often advertised with signs that suggest the end of the world like Grandes Rebajas! and Liquidación!

Canarian costume

The Canary Islands have had duty free status since 1852, but the casual shopper hoping for great bargains will be disappointed. Most of the benefits are for the import/export trade and unless you're a bulk shipper of bananas put away the plastic. 'Duty Free' is still bandied around the island's shops though, and in the resorts and Calle del Castillo in Santa Cruz you'll encounter emporia of 'Tax Free' bazaars selling cameras, watches, hi-fi and electrical goods. Most of these are run by Indians, a legacy of the island's long-standing free port status.

Unless you know exactly what you want and the item's relative price back home, it's unlikely you'll make a saving sufficient to justify the risks involved. Before you buy, have the product fully demonstrated, check that the guarantee is valid beyond the Canaries, and that there is an instruction manual in English. If prices are unmarked and you want to bargain, most traders will oblige.

Duty Free Allowances

In 1993 the European single market came into force, which means that for EU-residents there are no restrictions on the movement of excise goods carried by travellers between member states for their own personal use. However the Canary Islands, despite being Spanish provinces, are not considered members of the EU for these purposes.

The following tax-free allowances are only for people aged 17 and over.

Alcohol
Over 38.8 proof, 1 litre; or under 38.8 proof, 2 litres; or fortified or

sparkling wine, 2 litres; plus still table wine 2 litres.

Tobacco
200 cigarettes or 100 cigarillos or 50 cigars or 250gms tobacco.

Perfume
60cc

Other Goods
Up to a value of £145

Markets

The island's principal produce market – the place to come for wonderful cut flowers, local delicacies such as wine, cheeses and honey, and fresh bread and fruit for picnics – is in Santa Cruz, **Nuestra Señora de África** (see *Option 1, page 44*). There is also a produce market in Puerto de la Cruz opposite the bus station.

In the south of Tenerife, regular crafts markets are held in **Los Cristianos, Playa de las Américas** and **Torvìscas**.

Local Specialities

Cheese, figs, honey, almonds, *mojo* sauce and dried fruit are good buys. Look out for produce from the other islands too, such as cheese from El Hierro *(queso herreño)* and La Palma, and the palm honey *miel de palma* and cakes – such as its speciality, *torta de vilana* – from La Gomera.

Tenerife's Guajiro *ron* (sugar cane rum) and the darker, liqueur-like *ron miel,* made from sugar cane and honey, are both fiery island spirits. There are also local fruit liqueurs made from banana, orange, pineapple, cherry and even almonds. Local wines are sold in most supermarkets – Viña Norte is one of the best. The Canaries also have a long tradition of tobacco-growing, and cigars are still manufactured in La Laguna and Garachico – try a *palmero,* a hand-made cigar rolled in a whole leaf.

Although they are really more Spanish than Canarian, terracotta kitchenware, *paella* dishes, candle-holders, sangria jugs and stationery prove good value, attractive buys. For fabric and imported silks **El Kilo's** large store in Santa Cruz (Calle del Castillo 10) has bargains for those prepared to rummage. In the department and chain stores, Spanish shoes and and swimwear are particularly worth investigating.

Handicrafts

These are best bought at the point of origin. If you want to purchase some of Tenerife's outstanding embroidery *(bordados)* and threadwork *(calados)* produced on the island since the 17th century, head straight for **Casa de los Balcones** in La Orotava (*see Option 8, page 69*). The island's long tradition of open threadwork

lives on in this working embroidery school, which also has outlets in Santa Cruz and Puerto de la Cruz (see relevant Town Walks). The work is most commonly bought in the form of table linen (tablecloths with matching napkins), but blouses, collars and handkerchiefs are also sold. If you buy elsewhere watch out for cheap imitations imported from the Far East.

Other Spanish and Canarian handicrafts can be found in the state-run **Artespaña** in Santa Cruz and in **Casa Iriarte** in Puerto de la Cruz (see *Town Walks, pages 43–4 and 53 respectively*). Straw dolls

Bird of Paradise flower, emblem of the Canary Islands

in local costumes, wooden kitchen utensils, musical instruments, woven bags, knives, palm-leaf baskets and primitive Gomeran pottery are other things to look out for. La Calera pottery in Puerto de la Cruz (near San Antonio) has a good range of hand-made pots and bowls.

Craft fairs *(ferias artesanía)* are also common and worth visiting if you come across them, as they sometimes have stalls from the smaller islands. There is also a well-attended Handicrafts Fair in Garachico on the first Sunday of the month.

So They Want a Present From the Canaries...

Strelitzias, or 'Bird of Paradise' flowers, are a popular awkward object to take back on the plane. Adopted as the Canary Islands' official flower, these have a waxy plumage of leaves that slowly opens to a spectacular orange bloom similar to a bird's head. Bouquets of cut roses are another good buy – get them on the day you leave or from the airport. Packets of seeds from the island's exotic flora are also fun, but be sure to include some sunflowers (fairly easy to grow) to avoid disappointment if your other seeds fail to germinate.

The local banana liqueur, *cobana,* comes in a distinctive bottle shaped like a bunch of bananas and few people leave Tenerife without a miniature version at least. It usually ends up on pancakes, ice-cream or banana splits, a perfect fate. *Mojo* sauce is not sold everywhere but is well worth tracking down for anyone who likes spicy food. Look out too for South American curiosities that creep into the supermarkets, like Venezuelan chocolate and tinned products from Argentina.

For French and Spanish perfumes call into the English-speaking Perfumería Scarlata in Puerto de la Cruz, which is at Calle Nieves Ravelo 1 just north of the central Plaza de la Inglesia. If you are visiting La Gomera, look out for its black palm honey – delicious with bananas and ice cream.

Property

Every year thousands of visitors to Tenerife get the urge to count up their savings and splash out on a place in the sun. It's why much of the island is a building site and why timeshare touts – officially known as OPCs (Off Property Contacts) – plague the seafronts. Their offers of free gifts to married couples who might be interested in buying into a timeshare apartment (now also called co-ownership) are followed up with some hard, high-pressure selling that has got the business a bad name. If you're seriously interested then go, but if you're dreaming or just fancy the free champagne or walkman, don't bother.

That said, Tenerife has some excellent properties that really have made dreams come true for a lot of people, particularly the newly-retired, and every year over 20,000 Britons buy property here. If you do get smitten, take faith in the fact that there are far more honest developers and estate agents working on the island than newsworthy crooks. Play it safe and straight and you should have no complaints. Be sure to employ only an established, licensed and recommended estate agent, likewise for your solicitor and lawyer. Sign nothing until you have sought legal advice – help is available from the Institute of Foreign Property Owners, Apartado de lorreas 418. 3590 Altea, Alicante, Spain.

ENTER

Walking

For centuries many parts of Tenerife could only be reached by foot-paths and mule-tracks, ancient and well-trodden *caminos* that criss-crossed the island's mountains and *barrancos* and kept its far-flung communities together. Some of these have become the modern roads now careering around the island but many linger on, obsolete routes still used by farmers, foresters and adventurous tourists.

As a consequence, Tenerife is ideal for walking, an island packed with contrasting landscapes that offers its visitors everything from seaside strolls and forest trails to desert treks and mountain hikes. ICONA, Spain's nature conservation institute, has also organised many *senderos turísticos* (tourist paths), marked with yellow signs

and liberally sprinkled with picnic sites. The best area for these is the Orotava Valley which has a well-marked network of footpaths perfect for a gentle ramble though the pines – **La Caldera** is a good starting point (on the C821 from Puerto de la Cruz to Teide, turn left soon after the Aguamansa trout farm).

For the more energetic walker there are spectacular routes through the lavascapes of Teide and over the choppy mountains of Teno and Anaga. For more information, ICONA distribute free leaflets with maps of walks in the Orotava Valley and Anaga. Their Visitors Centre in the Parque Nacional del Teide also provides details for independent and guided walks around Las Cañadas. However, newcomers may find these maps confusing and it pays to invest in one of the countryside guides *Landscapes of Tenerife* (see *Information section, page 107*), which contain industriously detailed walks around the island.

Sport

Canary wrestling, or *lucha Canaria,* is Tenerife's favourite sport, a barefoot tussle between two men that developed from the duels and trials by combat of Guanche times. Matches are played all around the island in local sports halls and small purpose-built stadia known as *terreros*. These contain sand-covered rings 30–33ft (9–10m) in diameter, where the individual bouts *(bregas)* are fought. The aim of the sport is to force some part of your opponent's body (apart from the feet) into contact with the floor by whatever grip, lift, trip or shove might be successful.

These days, *lucha canaria* is played on a league basis with teams of 12 wrestlers competing. The easiest place to see it is in a bar, as matches are

often televised, but if you want to attend look for the posters advertising local games that regularly appear on walls and in bars, or ask at the local Tourist Office. Exhibition bouts are often held as part of a *fiesta* or *romería,* where you may also see some *juego de palo* or *banot,* a fast-moving form of stick-fighting that also dates from pre-Conquest days.

Basketball and **soccer** are also extremely popular – the island's principal football team is C.D. Tenerife. The team plays in the Heliodoro Rodriguez Stadium in Santa Cruz. In the south the local team, San Marino, attracts regular British support for its Sunday night matches in Playa de las Américas (the ground is situated next to the Clinica Las Américas).

At present there is no **bullfighting** in Tenerife because of prohibitive costs, but male Tinerfeños still indulge their machismo with cockfighting and hunting.

For **golf** the island has one course in the north near Guamasa, **Club de Golf El Peñon** (Tel: 25 02 40) and another two in the south on the Costa del Silencio – **Golf del Sur** (Tel: 70 45 55) and the **Amarilla Golf and Country Club** (Tel: 78 57 77). There are also several sports clubs in Playa de las Américas, Puerto de la Cruz and Los Gigantes which offer temporary membership, and many hotels have excellent sports, fitness and tennis facilities that

non-residents may hire. To find your nearest ask at a hotel reception or look for adverts in the local press.

Scuba diving is available in Los Gigantes (by the marina); deep-sea fishing trips are also run from here and Los Cristianos (see Option 6) – on one recent fishing expedition an English tourist landed a record 330lb (150kg) white shark.

Nightlife

For a good night out try the **Casino Taoro** in Puerto de la Cruz. Originally the Grand Hotel Taoro, it was built in 1892 as the flagship of the island's early tourist industry and became a favourite winter residence for European aristocracy up until 1929, when a fire destroyed much of the building and all of its reputation. Its prominent position among the lovely ornamental gardens of the Parque Taoro still guarantees an evening of compelling views over the bright lights of the north coast.

Now run by the Cabildo, the casino opens at 7pm and is well worth popping in, if only for a drink. Be sure to try a Cocktail Taoro – concocted from champagne, calvados, banana liqueur, lemon and caviar – as it won the 1988 Spanish National Cocktail Competition. There is also a restaurant, roulette and blackjack tables and some irresistible slot machines where a 100ptas coin could win you a 5,000,000ptas jackpot. The casino is at its liveliest around midnight and respectable dress is expected – admission is 500ptas and you must take your passport with you. There is also a smaller modern casino in Playa de las Américas, located next to the Hotel Gran Tinerfe.

Tenerife's nightclubs and discos pander to all tastes. Whether you're distinguished or depraved, if you like a drink and a dance there's always someone willing to stay up all night putting the records on. The most select venues often form part of a luxury hotel – such as the stylish **El Coto** in the **Hotel Botánico**, or combined with restaurants – like the **Tropical Palace** in San Antonio. Both of these nightclubs are in Puerto de la Cruz, where the nocturnal hi-jinks centre on the neon highway Avenida de Colón, its

neighbouring streets spangled with cafés, piano bars and disco-pubs. There is also a nightly international floorshow in the Lago Martiánez.

In Playa de las Américas the gaudy nerve-centre is **Veronicas,** a madness of discos and theme pubs where the night begins with Happy Hour at 11pm and jives on until dawn, with the party sometimes ending unhappily. If you prefer a more respectable evening, try large hotels like the **Bouganville Playa, Gran Tinerfe** and **Mediterranean Palace,** which often put on a little night music, sometimes with cabaret, or visit the **Orquidea Night Club**, which offers dinner-and-floorshow entertainment. There are also well-advertised all-in evening excursions where you can go, for example, on a beach barbecue or Latin American night.

If you want to escape the tourist complexes, Santa Cruz springs to life at the weekends—popular venues here are **Daida** and **Tinabana** (Residencia Anaga), **El Tropa** and **Chic** (Rambla del General Franco), while the bars along **Avenida Anaga** often stay open well into the night. You'll generally find entry to down-market discos is free, with admission only charged for more popular and select clubs – the price usually includes a free drink anyway. Always take taxis – at night the streets are paved with lunatics.

Calendar of Special Events

The Canarios have a joke that every day, somewhere in the Canary Islands, there's a fiesta going on. They're not far from the truth and its virtually impossible to visit Tenerife without encountering some celebration or holiday. The island leads the archipelago in the festivity stakes, with over 30 days of officially-sanctioned partying, many of which are well worth attending.

The biggest of them all takes place just before Lent, Santa Cruz's internationally-acclaimed *Carnaval* (see panel). Another big attraction is the floral carpets laid down in La Laguna and La Orotava in honour of Corpus Cristi. The religious calendar still sets the pace for most of the island's cele-

brations. The majority of these are *fiestas,* festivals often held in honour of a patron saint. Sometimes these are large-scale shindigs that go on for days, like those in honour of Our Lady of Carmen in Puerto de la Cruz, or they can be smaller local celebrations (often the most enjoyable for the casual visitor prepared to join in) in aid of a village's particular patron, such as for San Marcos (St Mark) in Icod.

Then there are the *romerías* or pilgrimages, traditionally rural events akin to our own harvest festivals. These tend to be passionate affairs with agricultural floats and garlanded oxen with local wine and produce lustily downed — your best chance to see the dark, superstitious side of Tinerfeño culture. There are also *ferias,* fairs often on a small scale that might be centred around a crafts or floral exhibition.

To the outsider such celebrations can seem chaotic affairs, the show sometimes stolen by politicians, Guanche

revivalists or hell-bent hedonists. But with luck you'll see some vibrant Canarian dancing, hear the Canarios' plaintive folk-songs and feel the pagan pulse beating beneath the imported histrionics of Catholicism. If possible go with a local or someone who knows what's happening, or ask at the Tourist Office for the time of the main event and the best place to stand. Take care too, for the crowds are disorganised, bonfires can get out of hand and spent fireworks may well rain on your head.

To find out what's on, look out for the colourful posters that warn of approaching fiestas – programmes are also listed in the local press or are available from Tourist Offices. The following calendar is only a guide and you should check dates before setting out – in Tenerife everything is a moveable fiesta.

Above and right: Santa Cruz Carnaval

January

The old year is normally seen off with a barrage of fireworks, car horns and ships' sirens. Revellers congregate in the main plazas or along the seafront, where the boats are often bedecked with lights colourful enought to rival the pyrotechnics rocketing into the night from inland villages.

Tradition says you should swallow a grape (and a sip of *cava* if you're quick enough) for each strike of the midnight clock. Needless to say, **Año Nuevo** (New Year's Day) is a necessary public holiday.

In Santa Cruz on the 5 January, the **Cabalgata del los Reyes Magos** (Calvacade of the Three Kings) celebrates the kings' coming with a colourful procession.

The following day (6 January) is a public holiday marking **Epiphany** (known elsewhere as Twelfth Night), the day when Spanish children finally get their Christmas presents.

On the 22 January there are also **local flestas** in Garachico, Icod and Los Realejos.

February

February means **Carnaval**, Tenerife's most engrossing celebration and well worth witnessing. It centres on Santa Cruz and Puerto de la Cruz, but as the month progresses party fever infects the whole island.

There are **local fiestas** in Candelaria on the 2nd (Candlemas) and in Güimar on the 7 February.

Franco banned carnivals in Spain but it didn't deter the *Santacruceros.* They ingeniously kept the party alive through the long years of his dictatorship by holding *Fiestas de Invierno,* Winter Festivals that have now blossomed into the extravagant Santa Cruz *Carnaval.* Today it's one of the world's top five carnivals and in 1987 the event earned itself a place in the *Guinness Book of Records* when more than 240,000 revellers packed into the Plaza de España to enjoy the largest carnival ball ever held.

If you are in Tenerife when it's on, go! It lasts up to 12 days, loosely pegged to Shrove Tuesday when its *Coso* or Grand Procession takes place. Other highlights are the Election of the Carnival Queen, when the brilliant, brainstorming costumes that it has taken all of the previous year to contrive are judged, and the Burial of the Sardine where widows mourn the death of a giant mock sardine that appears to have died from eating too many fireworks.

Every year follows a different theme (Ancient Egypt and Disneyland for example) and the Latin American influence is strong with processions *(comparsas)* of flamboyantly costumed dancers sambaing down the street in true Rio style, often accompanied by satirical groups of singers known as *murgas.* Full programmes are normally available from Tourist Offices and published in the local press – most events take place in the evening and if you want a seat to view the parades and floats you'll have to get there well in advance.

There are also plenty of sideshows, open-air concerts and wandering musicians as well as kiosks selling essential *carnaval* fare: *pinchitos* (kebabs), *pepitos* (steak rolls) and *churros* (doughnuts), which should be washed down with plenty of *cubatas* (rum and Coke).

March / April

March 19th is **San José** (St Joseph's Day), a public holiday. **Semana Santa** (Easter Holy Week) is a serious religious celebration with everything closed on Holy Thursday and Good Friday. On April 25th there are **local fiestas** in Icod and Tegueste.

May / June

On May 1st **Día del Trabajo** (Labour Day) is suitably marked by a day off work. In Santa Cruz this day also starts a month of celebration and cultural activity in honour of the capital, known as **Fiestas de Primavera** (Spring Festivals). In Los Realejos (15th) a festi-

pus Christi, Laguna

val in honour of **San Isidro** and Santa María de la Cabeza has a large **firework display**.

Corpus Christi (late May or early June) is another important Catholic celebration honoured throughout the island. In La Laguna and La Orotava the creation of long and intricate carpets of flowers are a spectacular act of homage well worth seeing. Months of planning lie behind these ornate tableaux that decorate the streets and plazas. Laboriously made from flower petals and the richly-coloured volcanic sands of Las Cañadas, they depict holy scenes that are lost forever once the solemn processions pass over.

Puerto de la Cruz fiesta

The end of the Octavo (Eight Days) of Corpus Christi marks the start of the *romeria* season, local fiestas with an agricultural flavour. The **Romería de San Isidro** in La Orotava (usually mid-June) and the **Romería de San Benito** in La Laguna (late June or early July) are two of the largest and best attended. During June there are also **local fiestas** in Granadilla, Güimar, Arico, Icod and El Sauzal.

July

In the week around the 15th Puerto de la Cruz holds its **Fiesta de la Virgen del Carmen,** a lively extravaganza with nautical games and regattas centred on its old fishing harbour. The next day (16th) there are *fiestas* in Los Realejos and Santa Cruz. The 25th is a public holiday, **Santiago Apóstol** (St.

Festival flowers

James' Day), in honour of Spain's patron saint. Santa Cruz celebrates the city's victory over Nelson and there are **fiestas** in Candelaria, Los Realjeos and Santiago del Teide. On the 27th La Laguna celebrates its patron saint, **San Cristóbal.**

August

The public holiday for **Asunción** (Assumption) on the 15 August coincides with the annual pilgrimage and *fiesta* in honour of the patroness of the Canarian archipelago, Nuestra Señora de la Candelaria. On that day the large square around its basilica (*see page 76*) is packed with thousands of devotees, who regularly come to the basilica from all the islands.

On the next day (16th) the **Romería de San Roque** takes place in the historic port of Garachico while on the 30th Los Cristianos honours **Nuestra Señora del Carmen.** Despite being in the centre of a tourist resort this *fiesta* still has bags of local atmosphere, with the taxi rank turned into a dance floor and a lively programme of games, processions and fireworks.

The Anaga mountains

September

In mid-September the *fiestas* celebrating **Santísimo Cristo** in La Laguna and Tacoronte coincide with the grape harvest. Their revels include cattle shows, displays of *lucha canaria,* fireworks and a veteran car rally round the island. There are also **local fiestas** in Güimar on the 7th and Guía de Isora on the 21st.

October

Christopher Columbus' discovery of America is celebrated on the 12th with a public holiday, **Día de la Hispanidad.** There is also a **local fiesta** in Granadilla.

November

On the 1st, **Todos los Santos** (All Saints' Day) is a public holiday.

December

Constitution Day on the 6th is a public holiday, followed closely by another on the 8th, **Inmaculada Concepción** (Immaculate Conception). **Navidad** (Christmas) is a traditional time for parties and cultural events. Tinsel and fairy lights decorate the pines while snowmen and reindeer hang incongruously from sun umbrellas. On Christmas Day (25th) turkey and mince pies on the beach fulfil many a winter holidaymaker's dream.

Watch out for the 28th too, when Spaniards celebrate their equivalent of April Fool's Day, **Día de los Inocentes** (Day of the Holy Innocents). On New Year's Eve, known to the Spanish as **Noche Vieja,** the Canarians throng the streets to celebrate the end of another year's fiestas, already plotting new ways to squeeze a few more into the next twelve months.

PRACTICAL Information

Tenerife may have begun as a 'winter sunshine' resort, but today the party never stops. November to April are the most popular months, with the price of flights and holidays peaking in the Christmas and Easter vacations. The summer months are more relaxed and a popular time for the mainland Spanish to visit. Many Tinerfeños take their holidays in June, the quietest month. If you want to catch the island's flora in its glory go between April and July, while the high spot of Tenerife's *fiesta*-filled calendar is the fortnight of *carnaval* that reaches its climax around Shrove Tuesday.

but altitude will affect you far more than season—there are often patches of snow on Teide as late as May.

Climate

'Over 2,500 sunshine hours a year' the brochures claim, and it's true if you're staying in the south of the island. Here rain is rare, though Saharan winds (the *sirocco*) may well turn your clear blue sky to a sandy haze, known locally as a *calima*. Tenerife's north coast is cooler and cloudier and the odd shower is the price you pay for its lush vegetation. Temperatures vary between 18°C (64°F) in January to 24°C (75°F) in August,

Where to Go

If sunshine is crucial, head for the southern coast. Its principal centres are Los Cristianos and Playa de las Américas, with smaller resorts illuminating the coast north to Los Gigantes and east along the Costa del Silencio. These are young holiday meccas that want fun and have it. Once brash, they are swiftly moving up-market with new marinas, golf courses and excellent windsurfing.

On the north coast, Puerto de la Cruz

has been entertaining tourists for over a century, its traditions now fostered by a lively resident British community. The resort is a good base for walks in the Orotava Valley and close to the island's historic capital, La Laguna. There are also several modern resorts scattered along the north coast, of which Bajamar is the largest.

Wherever you stay, all parts of the island can be easily reached in a day trip by hire car or taxi. If you intend to use public transport, avoid staying in the more isolated resorts.

How to Get There

Most likely, you will be one of the five million passengers who fly to Tenerife every year. The island is just under four hours from the UK: Iberia (Tel: 0171-830 0011) operates a scheduled service from Heathrow via mainland Spain while Monarch (Tel. 01582 398333) flies direct from Luton.

The majority of visitors to the island buy an all-in package deal that includes flight, accommodation and car hire – your local travel agent will be able to shower you with brochures for this type of holiday, by far the most economical way to see Tenerife. First Choice (Tel: 0161-745 7000) are a reputable example. Charter companies also offer flight-only deals – for the best offers, look in the classified section of the local and national newspapers. Most charter flights go on a Tuesday or Friday. Further savings can be made if you book outside the school holidays or at the last minute.

Tenerife's main international airport

is the modern Reina Sofía on the Costa del Silencio. A second northern airport, Los Rodeos, operates flights to the other Canary Islands.

You can also arrive by the weekly ferry from Cadiz, run by Trasmediterranea. Details from Southern Ferries, Tel: 0171-491 4968.

BEFORE YOU GO

Documents

You will need a valid passport and international driving permit.

Money

Traveller's cheques, Eurocheques and credit cards are all accepted. Get some pesetas before you go, especially if you're arriving late at night or plan to take a taxi to your hotel.

Health

No vaccinations are required but health insurance is recommended. Form E111, available from main post offices, entitles EU nationals to reciprocal medical benefits. Insect bites are rare, stomach upsets possible, hangovers inevitable. A strong sun cream is essential.

Clothing

Sunglasses, hat and swimming costume are enough for the beach but take something warm for the evenings and air-conditioned buildings. If you plan to do a lot of walking or climb Teide, take strong footwear and a jumper or anorak – there's snow at the summit! A jacket and tie aren't essential but the best of Tenerife's discos, clubs and casinos attract a smart crowd.

Electricity

220 volts. Sockets take round two-point plugs (European size) and most UK appliances will need an adaptor. A torch can be useful as power cuts do sometimes occur on the island.

Photography

Film is cheaper in the UK and some types can only be bought in the main cities. Develop it when you get home.

ON ARRIVAL

A taxi from Reina Sofía airport to Playa de las Américas costs 2000ptas and takes about 15 minutes; to Puerto de la Cruz it costs 9000ptas and takes around an hour and 45 minutes.

A regular TITSA bus service runs between the airport and Santa Cruz to

coincide with Iberia's scheduled flights from the mainland (line 341). To get to Puerto de la Cruz you'll have to change at Santa Cruz and take line 102. Buses to Los Cristianos and Playa de las Américas are infrequent and it's best to take a taxi.

Hire cars can also be collected at the airport (see *Getting Around*).

ON DEPARTURE

In recent years Tenerife has had its fair share of air traffic delays. To confirm your flight, telephone 75 92 00.

For Duty Free allowances see *Shopping*. The Duty Free shop in the airport is small and expensive, so make your purchases before you arrive.

WHERE TO STAY

It is usually cheapest to arrange an all-inclusive flight and accommodation package before you leave, plus car hire if you require it.

Virtually all Tenerife's tourist hotels are modern, with full facilities including air-conditioned rooms, a restaurant and swimming pool. When making a choice consider where the hotel is situated in the resort – those in the centre are convenient for the beach but can be noisy while those on the edge of town are more restful but can seem isolated. Many more hotels are currently being built, so don't be surprised if your guaranteed sea-view includes a panorama of the excavators working on the building site next door.

Hotels range from one-star to five-star. These are approximate prices for a double room with its own private bath in high season:

One-star, 4,000ptas
Two-star, 5,000ptas
Three-star, 6,000–8,000ptas
Four-star, 9,000–12,000ptas
Five-star, 20,000ptas.

For sheer glitz, try the five-star **Hotel Mediterranean Palace de Luxe** in Playa de las Américas (Avenida del Litoral, Tel: 79 25 05), while the three-star **Hotel Marquesa** in Puerto de la Cruz (Quintana 15, Tel: 38 46 11), built in 1712, has true Canarian character. Tenerife also has a state-run hotel, currently being upgraded to become the four-star **Parador Nacional de las Cañadas del Teide** (Tel: 33 23 04), spectacularly located in the heart of the ancient caldera beside Teide volcano –

you should book well ahead. Self-catering apartments *(apartamentos turisticos)* are also popular and best booked through a travel agent. The minimum stay is normally a week. Outside the package holiday scene, cheap accommodation in *hostales* and *pensiones* is limited – a list can be obtained from the Tourist Office. There is one official campsite at **Nauta Camping**, Cañada Blanca, Arona, Tel: 78 51 18.

Driving

Drive on the right and take care – in recent years there's been a horrific rise in the number of fatal traffic accidents on the island. Use of seatbelts is obligatory and motoring offences are rewarded with on-the-spot fines. Some petrol stations are closed on Sundays and public holidays and not all of them take credit cards. In a courageous attempt to suppress the Spanish love of

GETTING AROUND

Car Hire

There are so many 'Rent-a-car' signs in Tenerife you'd think they held the buildings up. Even so it can still be hard to get a car at peak times like Christmas, so if you know your requirements, book before you go. Prices are from around 3,500ptas a day with insurance (800ptas) and tax on top. Take your passport and international driving licence – most firms will not rent to drivers under 21 or with less than a year's experience. Motorbikes can also be rented in larger resorts.

triple parking, Blue Zones (Zonas Azul) have been installed in busy streets in Puerto de la Cruz, Santa Cruz and Playa de las Américas. If parking in these areas you need to pay-and-display a ticket bought from machines nearby. Check the designated times, usually weekdays 9am–2pm and 4–8pm

Touring

Buy a sunshade to cover your windscreen and keep your car interior cool. Try to do your Island Tour during the week when the roads are less busy and take your swimming things – you're on an island and the chance for a dip

Santa Cruz. A bus is a *guagua* and a stop a *parada*. Free maps and timetables are available from main termini, but if you ride into the hills double-check your return with the driver. The island's central bus station is in Avenida Tres de Mayo, Santa Cruz, Tel: 21 56 99.

Coach Tours

Many travel agents and hotels on Tenerife advertise coach trips. Their half-, full-day and evening excursions offer an easy, collective way to see Tenerife's main attractions. If you want to avoid driving and don't mind the loss of independence, try the round island tours and visits to scenic sights like Teide, Masca and La Gomera.

Taxi Tours

Touring the island or visiting its sights by taxi is a comfortable and pleasant way to see Tenerife. If there are several of you it can be quite economical, though always agree a price before setting off.

Sample fares for four-passenger trips from Puerto de la Cruz:
Orotava Valley (two hours), 3,500ptas;
Island Tour (7 hours), 9,000ptas.
From Playa de las Américas:
Teide (6 hours), 8,000ptas;
Anaga (8 hours), 11,000ptas;
Island Tour (9 hours); 11,000ptas.

constantly arises. Be sure to have a picnic at least one day – Tenerife has many beach and forest picnic sites, ideal for a long walk and a lazy *merienda*.

Taxis

Tenerife's taxis are fair and efficient and most are metered. A green *libre* sign or light indicates availability for hire. Agree on a price first for long journeys or tours. To call a taxi:
Playa de las Américas, Tel: 79 14 07.
Los Cristianos, Tel: 79 03 52.
Puerto de la Cruz, Tel: 38 49 10.
Rest of the island, Radio Taxi-7-Islas, Tel: 61 51 11.

Buses

An extensive and popular bus service unites the island. TITSA is the main company, with distinctive green buses that are mostly new and air-conditioned. Their express routes along the *autopistas* from Puerto de la Cruz (line 102) or Playa de las Américas (line 111) are well worth using, ideal for a day trip into

INFORMATION

Tourist Offices

London: Spanish National Tourist Office, 57–58 St James St, London SW1. Tel: 0171-499 0901.

Santa Cruz: Palacio Insular, Plaza de España. Tel: 60 58 00.

Puerto de la Cruz: Plaza de la Iglesia 3. Tel: 38 60 00.

Playa de las Américas: Urbanización Torviscas, Tel: 75 06 33.

Los Cristianos: By the Town Hall. Tel: 75 24 92

Las Galletas: Avenida Maritima, Tel: 73 01 33.

Playa de la Arena: Centro Comercial Seguro del Sol, Avenida Maritima, Tel: 11 03 48.

Tourist Offices are generally open at least 9am–6pm Monday–Friday and 9am–noon on Saturdays. Those in Santa Cruz, Puerto de la Cruz and Playa de las Américas stay open during the lunch hours.

Media

Several English language newspapers and magazines offer insightS into island life and contain 'What's On' sections, available in newsagents' kiosks. Look for the fortnightly newspaper *Island Sun*, the free monthly *Tenerife Holiday Gazette*, and *Island Connections*. Daily English newspapers can be bought in the resorts on the afternoon of publication.

Bookshops

Upstairs at **Librería Goytec** in Santa Cruz (Calle Pérez Galdós 15, Tel: 24 53 14) you'll find a wide range of books on the Canary Islands in English and Spanish, including guides to their flora, ornithology and volcanic origins. The **Visitors' Centre** in the **Parque Nacional del Teide** also has a good selection.

Reading

Insight Guide: Tenerife and the Western Canary Islands offers in-depth essays on Tenerife past and present and introduces the smaller islands of La Gomera, La Palma and El Hierro. Includes lavish photography, maps and a detailed travel tips section.

Natural History Excursions in Tenerife by Myrtle and Philip Ashmole (Kidston Mill Press) is a detailed guide to the island's landscape, plants and animals and includes 24 nature-spotting walks. Noel Rochford's *Landscapes of Tenerife* and *Landscapes of Southern Tenerife and La Gomera* (Sunflower) are practical guides to walking and picnicking on the island.

Tipping and Service

Tipping is normal but not obligatory – 10 percent for taxi-drivers and restaurants, at least 50ptas for hotel staff and waiters. Some restaurants will add a service charge but many people still leave a tip. In bars it generally costs more if you sit down at a table and

Banks

Banks are more punctual than shops and open 9am–2pm Monday–Friday, 9am–1pm Saturday. Money can also be changed at hotels and travel agents. Remember to take your passport with you. 'Hole-in-the-wall' cashpoint facilities are common in the resorts and main towns.

are served by a waiter. You pay the bill *(la cuenta)* at the end – unless of course you're in an English pub, when you pay as you drink.

Time Difference

For most of the year there is no time difference between Britain and Tenerife. In winter the Canary Islands follow Greenwich Mean Time and in summer (April to September) they observe the changeover to Summer Time. Sometimes there is a discrepancy of a few weeks when the two countries change their clocks over on different dates. Mainland Spain is normally one hour ahead.

Business Hours

Canarian opening hours often seem to depend on what happened the night before, but everything generally makes a start at around 9am. Things then stop at 1pm – the Spanish day is traditionally divided by a long lunch and a siesta, a practice well worth observing. Business resumes again about 4.30pm and continues till 7 or 8pm. Some government offices work through until 3pm and do not re-open. You'll also find that in the resorts some shops and supermarkets keep longer hours, while up in the mountains there are villages that don't appear to have opened up for the last 20 years.

Post Offices

Open 9am–2pm Monday–Friday, 9am–1pm Saturday, but avoid them if you can. Stamps *(sellos)* can be bought in tobacconists and most hotel receptions. A postcard to the UK *(Reino Unido)* costs 60ptas, as does a letter up to 20gm.

Museums

Usually open at least 10am–1pm and 4–6pm, sometimes closed for one weekday. See individual entries.

Public Holidays

The more *fiestas* the Tinerfeños can pack into the calendar the happier they are. Those traditionally shared with the mainland are supplemented by a heavy timetable of Canary Island celebrations, with village feast days thrown in whenever things seem to be getting too quiet. See *Special Events* for details and don't be surprised if the party goes on longer than planned.

Toilets

Don't waste time looking for public conveniences, they're few and far between. Pop into a bar, hotel or restaurant and use the *servicios* (sometimes marked *aseos*) – you don't have to be a customer but it's polite to ask first. Sorting out the *Señoras* and *Damas* (women) from the *Señores, Hombres* and *Caballeros* (men) is more tricky – the Spanish seem to put all their energy into designing obscure silhouettes and coy cartoons to put on the doors and don't always bother about what lies beyond them.

Health

'In winter, when the volcano is covered with ice and snow, an eternal spring prevails here. In summer, towards evening, the sea wind brings agreeable coolness.' So wrote Alexander von Humboldt following his visit in 1799, and Tenerife still has a justified reputation as a health resort, a sunshine isle with refreshing sea breezes and mountain air. It has few natural hazards and no poisonous snakes or insects. Strong winds can make some beaches unsafe for swimming and if you've a heart or respiratory complaint it would be inadvisable to make the ascent to Teide's summit.

Most health problems are man-made, over-indulgence being a popular source of misery that invariably results from a disrespect for the large measures of cheap spirits available here. Beware the sun's beguiling strength too, as it's very easy to get burnt, even up in the mountains. Insect bites can occur so take a cream or repellent. Always drink bottled water.

For minor problems, chemists *(farmacias)* are a good source of advice. Unlike our own they're devoted solely to dispensing medication and are marked by a green cross outside. Don't confuse them with *droguerías,* which sell perfume and toiletries. *Farmacias* are open shop hours with a rota of after-hours service *(farmacia de guardia)* – to find this look for a sign in the window or telephone 28 24 24.

For a doctor *(médico)* or dentist *(dentista)* ask at a hotel or Tourist Office or look for their adverts in the local press (see *Information* above). Many speak English, some are English and their service is generally prompt. State facilities are adequate but often slower. For British citizens, Form E111 issued by the DSS entitles you to certain benefits but you must first get treatment vouchers from its Spanish equivalent, the **Instituto Nacional de la Seguridad Social (INSS),** and you can then only go to doctors who operate the scheme. Good medical insurance is a far better bet.

Centro Medicas Salus Canarias offer private medical facilities with a 24-hour English-speaking service and British insurance accepted.

They have centres in Puerto de la Cruz, La Orotava, Los Gigantes and Playa de las Américas. Freefone information, Tel: 900 100144.

EMERGENCIES

To call the police and other emergency services dial 091.
To call an ambulance:
Playa de las Américas, Tel: 78 07 59.
Puerto de la Cruz, Tel: 38 38 12.

You may also go to a first aid station *(casa de socorro),* obvious from their familiar red cross insignia.
To call the Fire Brigade:
Playa de las Américas,Tel: 71 08 80.
Puerto de la Cruz, Tel: 33 00 80.

Police

Policemen come in three colours. In urban areas the **Policia Nacional** (wearing brown uniforms) rule the streets while the **Policia Municipal** (wearing blue uniforms with white caps) control the traffic. The **Guardia Civil** (green with tricorn hats) rule everything else. Despite the shades and swaggers they're all quite helpful.

Trouble

The Canarios are quiet, family-loving people who seem remarkably tolerant of the four million tourists who descend on their islands every year. Compared to some Spanish (or British) cities, Tenerife remains a safe and trouble-free island, though crime is on the increase. Visiting foreigners account for a good deal of the petty thefts and drugs-related crimes committed here, so vigilance and common sense precautions are especially important in cities and resorts. In particular, don't carry large sums of money or valuable documents in pockets or handbags, take nothing to the beach and never leave anything you care about in a car. Use hotel safes, lock balcony doors when you go out and be adequately insured.

The police keep a high profile in the resorts, patrolling popular beaches by day and controlling unpopular yobs all night. Timeshare touts often pester tourists along the seafront – if you don't want to talk to them just keep on walking.

Should anything untoward happen to you, tell your hotel or holiday representative, who should then help you inform the police and make a statement for insurance purposes. If you are travelling independently try to enlist the help of a resident who can interpret for you. If you lose your passport, contact your consulate.

Consulates

British Consulate, Plaza Weyler 8, 1st floor, Santa Cruz, Tel: 28 68 63.
Irish Consulate, La Marina 7, Santa Cruz, Tel: 24 56 71.
US Consulate, Alvarez de Lugo 10, Santa Cruz, Tel: 28 69 50.

Telephone

The Spanish telephone system is good, so good the net effect is bad. Too many people want to use it, coinboxes fill up quickly, at peak times it can be hard to get a line anywhere, at Christmas impossible.

Fortunately, there are plenty of phone boxes around. Those marked *Telefónica Internacional* can be used to call abroad – remember to stock up with 100, 200 or 500ptas coins first. They also take 25 and 50ptas coins, which you should use for local calls. Better still, visit one of the *cabinas* scattered around the main towns and resorts – multi-boothed centres where your calls are metered by an assistant whom you pay at the end. Most are open from 9am–1pm and 4–9pm.

All public phone boxes have clear instructions in English, French and German about international dialling. First dial 07, followed by the country's code:
UK 44
Eire 353
France 33
Germany 49
Australia 61
USA and **Canada** 1

If using a US credit phone card, dial the company's access number below –
Sprint: 900 99 0013
AT&T: 900 99 00 11
MCI: 900 99 0014.

An engaged tone sounds like a rapid beeping, and the number for the operator is 003.

Facilities for the Disabled

Tenerife has become popular as a holiday resort for disabled travellers, who are attracted by its invigorating climate and ready access to modern medical facilities. The newer hotels tend to be the most accommodating and the level promenades and seafronts of Playa de las Américas and Los Cristianos are particularly suited for disabled holidaymakers. However, provisions vary widely across the island – there are still only a few purpose-built toilets or telephone kiosks, for instance.

Some package holiday operators offer holidays to hotels in the main resorts that can cater for disabled travellers. Your travel agent will be able to advise, but be sure to tell them the nature and extent of your disability.

For more information on travelling as a disabled person, consult the Royal Association for Disability and Rehabilitation's annual handbook *Holidays and Travel Abroad,* available from RADAR, 250 City Road, London EC1V 8AF. Tel: 0171-250 3222.

The charity Holiday Care Service is also a useful source of information: for details, write to 2nd Floor, Imperial Buildings, Victoria Road, Horley, Surrey RH6 7PZ. Tel: 01293 774535.

Children

Tenerife is ideal for children. Not only does it offer safe family holidays by the sea and a madness of exhausting amusements and diversions, it actually likes them. Like the mainland Spanish, the Canarios think that children should be seen, heard and utterly spoilt. Here they're not just tolerated but enjoyed, welcome guests in bars and restaurants and a surefire way to meet the locals.

Package holiday hotels can provide cots and high chairs (book ahead), while baby food, nappies, powdered milk and other necessities are available in supermarkets. Take a maximum-strength sun cream, hat and sun umbrella. The larger hire-car firms can supply child car seats but order well in advance at peak times and take a sun-screen for the windows. In Spain it is against the law for children under 12 to travel in front seats.

Babysitters can be arranged through hotels – try to give as much notice as you can, as availability varies. Tourist Offices have details of private services.

Religion

Like Spain, the Canary Islands are Roman Catholic. Some religious centres regularly hold services in English; their details are often advertised in the local press. In Puerto de la Cruz there is an Anglican Church, All Saints' in Parque Taoro.

Art & Photo Credits

10 **Tony McCann**

13, 14, 66, 76, 78t and 78b **Andrew Eames**

79 **Mary Tisdall**
28, 29, 33b. 39, 44, 63t, 63b, 67 80, 83t, 83b, 84 **Nigel Tisdall**
85, 86, 89, 93, 102, 105, 108, 110, 111
2/3, 8/9 **Bill Wassman**

3, 22, 36, 49, 50, 53, 87, 88, 95, 97 (both), 98 **La Antigua Casa de la Real Aduana**
99 (both), 100, 101

Cover design **Klaus Geisler**
Cartography **Berndtson & Berndtson**

The author would like to thank the following individuals and organisations for their help and assistance:
Fuji Photo Film (UK) Ltd; Gloria Salgado de Reyes and the Patronato de Turismo in Santa Cruz; Monarch
Airlines; Viajes Insular SA, Playa de las Américas; OCCA Car Rental; First Choice Holidays; Austin Baillon;
Mary and Archie Tisdall; Alice, Viv, Lilia and Claudia.